IN SEARCH OF THE FATHER

Two Plays

ANITA S. CHAPMAN

CHIRON PUBLICATIONS • ASHEVILLE, NORTH CAROLINA

www.ChironPublications.com

Interior and cover design by Danijela Mijailovic
Printed primarily in the United States of America.

ISBN 978-1-68503-052-0 paperback
ISBN 978-1-68503-053-7 hardcover
ISBN 978-1-68503-054-4 electronic
ISBN 978-1-68503-055-1 limited edition paperback

Library of Congress Cataloging-in-Publication Data

Names: Chapman, Anita S., author.

Title: In search of the father : two plays / Anita S. Chapman.

Description: Asheville, North Carolina : Chiron Publications, 2022. | Includes bibliographical references. | Summary: "When the archetypal patriarchal or matriarchal dominate in a daughter's psyche, the positive masculine spirit does not mature sufficiently out of the maternal unconscious for there to be an optimal meeting between feminine and masculine principles. It becomes difficult for a more conscious, well-integrated, whole human being to develop. Where inadequate or incompetent fathering is combined with absent or passive, silent mothering, the balance is off; a daughter's talents and possibilities for the future can remain dormant-or fade away in self-doubt. These analytical discussions of two plays, The Heiress and A Delicate Balance, demonstrate how too much or too little parenting can have this detrimental effect. Particularly, when a father withdraws from the family and does not give loving attention to his daughter, or when he presents himself as an overbearing elder, he is neglecting to support his child in the natural process of separation from the mother/Mother-not helping her achieve personal autonomy and an individual life of her own. As an adult, such a daughter will likely find herself in a place not directed from within by her unique potential for wholeness, but rather in one dictated by the limiting expectations of her family and the collective patriarchal culture around her"-- Provided by publisher.

Identifiers: LCCN 2022024509 (print) | LCCN 2022024510 (ebook) | ISBN 9781685030520 (paperback) | ISBN 9781685030537 (hardcover) | ISBN 9781685030544 (ebook)

Subjects: LCSH: Fathers and daughters--Psychological aspects. | Daughters-- Psychology. | Archetype (Psychology) | Goetz, Ruth. Heiress. | Albee, Edward, 1928-2016. Delicate balance.

Classification: LCC BF723.F35 C43 2022 (print) | LCC BF723.F35 (ebook) | DDC 155.9/24--dc23/eng/20220613

LC record available at https://lccn.loc.gov/2022024509

"Every single 'too much' or 'too little' which falls beyond the appropriate range will be experienced as negative by the child."

- *Erich Neumann*

Dedication

For my Father
Karl Stenz
In Loving Memory

Contents

Preface

In analytical work, paternal deprivation is often a major issue for women, as well as for men. My particular interest in the quality of the father/daughter relationship began early, when, among my very first analysands, there were two women who told me their fathers were not important to them. They each started their analysis insisting that talking about their male parent was not relevant to their presenting problems. It soon became clear these women lacked a personal relationship with their fathers. Emotionally detached from them, they were woefully disconnected from the positive heroic and spiritual *masculine* principles, which the archetypal Father, who stands behind the personal father, represents. Both women suffered from depression and anxiety, as well as dependency conflicts and crises in relationships.

Traditionally, typically, the first man in a woman's life is her biological father. In a patriarchal culture, it can be anticipated that the way a father looks at his daughter will have lasting effects on the value she gives to herself, as well as on the kind of relationships she has with men. Perhaps the

1

most insidious and deleterious consequence an emotionally absent or an emotionally hostile father can have is that— unwittingly or maliciously—he undermines his daughter's sense of self-worth as a physical and spiritual human being in a world of men and women.

To illuminate psychological issues that come up during a consultation, it has always felt natural to me to bring stories— especially plots and situations from dramatic literature and film—into my conversations with analysands. Supported by a Jungian lens, my intention in this book is to interpret and discuss the archetypal dynamic behind the father/daughter relationships in two prize-winning twentieth-century American plays: *The Heiress* by Ruth and Augustus Goetz and *A Delicate Balance* by Edward Albee. Using the father/daughter conflicts in these two dramas as examples, I will illustrate how a father's negative attitudes and reactions can have an adverse effect on the psyche of his daughter, and become an inhibiting influence which prevents her from developing into a whole woman—one who is independent and competent to take care of herself in the world.

Over the years it has been analysands who have been the well-spring for my curiosity about father/daughter issues. When I presented some of this material at the International Seminar for Analytical Psychology in Zurich, students were most receptive; they inspired me to think more about the subject and to write this book. Special gratitude goes to my colleagues and friends, Nathalie Baratoff, Barbara Hess Kovaz, Patricia and Terrence Lee, and Pedro Kujawski for their interest in my project, and for their insightful and supportive comments. I am indebted to Ellen Aldrich and to Mike L. and Carol Cole Czeczot for their valuable editorial assistance.

"There is no justification for visualizing the archetype as anything other than the image of instinct in man."

- C.G. Jung

Introduction:
Myth and Culture

1.

In Iran recently, a father beheaded his daughter while she was sleeping because he discovered she was planning to run away with a man he didn't approve of.[1] Whatever the specific details of the circumstances were, as Westerners we are appalled—outraged—to hear of such barbaric behavior. Yet, we do it all the time. If we step back a little, if we look at the act not concretely but psychologically and emotionally, we can say that fathers have been cutting off their daughters' heads with conviction since antiquity. Metaphorically and symbolically, over the centuries it has not been unusual for a father, or what he represents—authority—to stand in the way of a daughter thinking for herself and developing into who she is humanly and individually capable of becoming. It is an archetypal dynamic.

---

[1] Farnaz Fassihi, "A Daughter is Beheaded and Iran Asks if Women Have a Right to Safety," *The New York Times*, June 7, 2020.

As C.G. Jung saw it, the collective unconscious contains "...the totality of all archetypes, is the deposit of all human experience right back to its remotest beginnings . . . a living system of reactions and attributes that determine the individual's life in invisible ways—all the more effective because invisible."[2] Jung describes the collective unconscious as a historical mirror image of the world: "It too is a world, but a world of images which is part of the collective psyche of every individual."[3] *"Archetypes are typical modes of apprehension, and wherever we meet with uniform and regularly recurring modes of apprehension we are dealing with an archetype, no matter whether its mythological character is recognized or not."*[4]

Looking back to antiquity, to the poet Hesiod, who was living around the time of Homer, and reading *Theogony,* his history of the birth of the world and the gods, we learn about two pre-Olympian deities who effectively beheaded their daughters, as well as their sons: Ouranos, who prevented his children from being born, and Kronos, who ate them alive.[5] I am going to explore, in particular, the archetypal phenomenon of fathers who have this not unfamiliar mindset when it comes to their daughters. Of course, then—for good and for bad—there was the king of the Olympian gods, Zeus, who did grant

---

[2] C.G. Jung, "The Structure of the Psyche," *The Structure and Dynamics of the Psyche*, CW 8, par. 339.
[3] C.G. Jung, "The Structure of the Unconscious," *Two Essays on Analytical Psychology*, CW 7, par. 507.
[4] C.G. Jung, "Instinct and the Unconscious," *The Structure and Dynamics of the Psyche*, CW 8, par. 280. (*Italics* are Jung's.)
[5] *Hesiod: Theogony, Works and Days, Shield*, Translation, Introduction, and Notes by Apostolos N. Athanassakis (Baltimore: John Hopkins University Press, 1983).

some of his daughters what they wanted. Parenthetically, I will also raise the question, where are the mothers?

Hesiod ranks among the earliest poets and teachers of the human race; he belongs to that transitional period when the oral tradition was giving way to the written. Apostolos N. Athanassakis, professor emeritus in the Department of Classical Studies at the University of California at Santa Barbara, estimates *Theogony* was composed sometime during the last quarter of the 8th century BC and believes that, "Much like Homer's epics, [it] must stand not at the beginning but at the apex of [the Hellenic] tradition." Hesiod, in his cosmography, gives his listeners and eventually his readers not only the compelling story of the birth of the Olympian gods, but also of the creation of the world and all the heavenly beings, monstrous and fair, who dwell within it. Although the theme of this 1,022-line poem is the birth of the gods, coming out of the poet's own "fiercely patriarchal" society, more than half of *Theogony* is devoted to the solid historical establishment of the supremacy of Zeus. And, as Athanassakis puts it, "There is nothing in Hesiod's world… that is not divine."[6]

Hesiod gives us the succession myth. He introduces the stories of Gaia and Ouranos, Rhea and Kronos, and of Zeus and his first wife, Metis; he vividly demonstrates the progress of the evolution from Chaos to Law. Athanassakis does not believe Hesiod changed the core of the traditional myths "… but rather the detail and the schematic arrangement."[7]

---

[6] See *Hesiod: Theogony*, Introduction, 1-11.
[7] *Theogony,* Notes, 50.

According to Hesiod, the first unions of the deities were primarily about procreation. Ouranos, fearful that one day he would be superseded by a powerful son, obstructed his children's birthing:

> ...for as soon as each one came from the womb,
> Ouranos with joy in his wicked work, hid it
> In Gaia's womb and did not let it return to the light.[8]

Eventually, full of anger, Gaia—who wanted the fruits of her creative efforts to be acknowledged—rebelled. She appealed to her son Kronos to help her. The next time "starry" Ouranos descended from the sky to couple with Gaia, with the sickle his mother gave him, Kronos quickly and effectively castrated his father and then emerged to become the next king.

A Titan goddess, Rhea, succumbed to Kronos's love and bore him illustrious children:

> However, Kronos soon realized
> ...that he, despite his own powers, was fated
> to be subdued by his own son, a victim of
> his own schemes.
> Therefore, he kept no blind watch, but ever wary
> he gulped down his own children to
> Rhea's endless grief.
> In time, Rhea appealed to her mother for help.

---

[8] This verse and the following quotations are from the poem *Theogony*, trans. Apostolos Athanassakis (Baltimore: John Hopkins University Press, 1983), 13-38.

When Zeus was born, his grandmother, Gaia, was on the spot to snatch the baby and hide him away:

> But to the great Lord Kronos, king of the older gods,
> (Rhea) handed a huge stone wrapped in swaddling clothes.
> He took it in his hands and stuffed it into his belly—
> the great fool! It never crossed his mind that the stone
> was given in place of his son thus saved to become
> carefree and invincible, destined to crush him by might of hand,
> drive him out of his rule, and become king of the immortals.

Yes, and when it was his time, Zeus defeated Kronos, destroyed the insurgent Titans and eliminated all possible rivals. He pursued and married his first wife, the pre-Olympian Titan goddess, Metis, whom Hesiod describes as "...a mate wiser than all gods and mortal men." Metis means resourcefulness and wisdom. Intelligence! When it was prophesied that she
"...would bear keen minded children,"

> (Zeus) deceived the mind of Metis with guile
> and coaxing words, and lodged her in his belly.

When her husband swallowed her, Metis was pregnant with a brilliant daughter. Therefore, the king of Olympus brought forth the powerful Athena himself—from his head—full grown. Being a female, though, there was no danger this goddess, however well-armed, would threaten his throne. Decisively, Zeus ensured that Metis would never bear "…a male child, high mettled and destined to rule over gods and men." He took his first wife totally into himself and assimilated her, "...that she might advise him in matters good and bad." As Athanassakis puts it, "Since by implication, none of the other wives of Zeus is like Metis, the danger of getting a son more resourceful than himself is permanently eliminated." Hesiod shows us how Zeus turned a Great Goddess into something small and—except as the invisible power behind the throne—silenced her.

We see in the imagery of the verses from *Theogony* the launching of enduring archetypal motifs: the rivalry between Father and Son, the plotting between Mother and Son against Father, the polarization of Puer and Senex, the collusion of Mother and Daughter against Father, and the swallowing of the *feminine* by the Patriarchy.

In these earliest writings of Western civilization, the shepherd poet, Hesiod, also establishes the concept of misogyny. To avenge Prometheus for stealing fire, "…[Zeus] contrived an evil for men—Woman!" He has the craftsman, Hephaestus, mold this meant-to-be mixed blessing from clay "…in the shape of a modest maiden." It is the woman of intellect, the father's daughter, Athena, who dresses her. (In his poem, is Hesiod setting up an archetypal divide among women who are different types?) Athena "…clothed her and decked her out with a flashy garment... crowned her head with lovely wreaths of fresh flowers..."

> Immortal gods and mortal men
> were amazed when they saw this tempting snare
> from which men cannot escape...
> yes, wicked womenfolk are her descendants.
> They live among mortal men as a nagging burden...
> And (Zeus) bestowed another gift, evil in place of good:
> whoever does not wish to marry, fleeing the malice of women,
> reaches harsh old age with no one to care for him...

Apostolos N. Athanassakis points out the following lines in Hesiod's later long poem, *Works and Days*, perhaps written in reconsideration of his earlier unkind indictments of women: "...nothing is better for a man than a good wife/and no horror matches a bad one." Athanassakis comments, "It may, in the final analysis, be the antithetic relationship, which is a precondition for symbiotic attraction, the negation that is a precondition of affirmation."[9] His words suggest Jung's theory of *the tension of opposites* and the need for the development of a *transcendent function*—a third thing.[10] Negotiation?

---

[9] See *Theogony*, 50.
[10] See *"Definitions,"* Psychological Types, CW 6, par. 824: "Since life cannot tolerate a standstill, a damming up of vital energy results, and this would lead to an insupportable condition did not the tension of opposites produce a new uniting function that transcends them."

Compromise? In any case, on the subject of archetypal dynamics, by the eighth century BC gender inequality and the battle of the sexes had well begun. Up to the present day, even with recent shifts in attitudes and reactions—and in spite of noticeable gains—resistance to change and backlash persist. We recognize there are still many subtle and not so subtle political, psychological and emotional ways to cut off a woman's head—or try to.

2.

Jung explains to us that "…behind the father stands the archetype of the Father, and in this pre-existent archetype lies the secret of the father's power…"[11] Ever on the lookout for archetypal patterns, I have found it helpful during an early session with an analysand to have Hesiod's ancient stories of the Olympian succession myth in mind. If I ask a woman to tell me about her relationship with her father, I can anticipate several different answers. One might say, with a dismissive wave of the hand, "Not important." Another, in a deferential tone, may reply, "My father was a god to me." It is not unusual to get an angry response like "I hated my father." Only occasionally in my practice have I heard a woman answer the question in a loving tone.

I remember a story an analysand told about a conversation she overheard when she was a teenager, between

---

[11] C.G. Jung, "The Father in the Destiny of the Individual," *Freud and Psychoanalysis*, CW 4, par. 739.

her grandfather and her mother. Her grandfather was saying he didn't believe in higher education for women—that when a woman graduated from college, she couldn't even boil water. Fortunately, this girl had a mother who went out to work so the family could afford to send their daughter to college. We can see a connection here between the mentality of this grandfather and that of the pre-Olympian Titan god, Ouranos, who deprived his children of the light of consciousness deliberately.

I'm reminded too of a client whose favorite class in high school was biology. When she told her father she wanted to become a biology teacher, he laughed. "Teachers don't make money," he said. "I'm not going to pay tuition for you to become a teacher." When the time came, her mother said, "Don't disappoint your father." This dutiful daughter got an advanced degree in business. She made a lot of money but working in the field gave her no pleasure. Echoes of her story suggest a father connecting back to the pre-Olympian god, Kronos, who, to be confident his children would yield only to his opinions and his values, devoured them whole.

Throughout *Theogony*, Hesiod has many names for Zeus: Olympian king of gods and men, aegis-bearer, and counselor, as well as cloud gatherer, roaring thunder and lightning. Once an analysand told me that when she shared with her father, who was a prestigious musician, how much she loved Vivaldi's *Four Seasons*, instead of supporting the adolescent girl's developing taste for classical music, he snapped disdainfully, "Popular stuff. Superficial. You should listen to Bach!" To her, his response was like a thunderbolt, a crippling flash of lightning. Feeling shamed and flawed, she lost her interest in serious music for a long time.

Then there was the analysand who, when she was a college student, was interested in many subjects. One day she said to her father, "I don't know yet what I want to be." Her father's reply was "Beauty is its own excuse for being." You can imagine this woman's difficulty adjusting to her aging process—when she didn't look twenty-one anymore. Jung has pointed out that "...every father is given the opportunity to corrupt, in one way or another, his daughter's nature..."[12]

These are just a few simple, very ordinary, everyday-life examples of what we mean by the archetypal negative reactions and attitudes of a father towards a daughter, which do not communicate his confidence that she can competently manage her life in her own individual way. They also illustrate how a daughter, who unknowingly experiences the archetypal Negative Father in her interactions with her personal father, is negatively affected. As Jung says, "The personal father inevitably embodies the archetype, which is what endows his figure with its fascinating power."[13]

We do know Zeus could also be encouraging to a daughter—a Positive Father. In his essay, "A Mythological Image of Girlhood," Karl Kerenyi quotes a charming passage from the "Hymn to Artemis" by the second-century Greek poet, Callimachus:

---

[12] C.G. Jung, "The Personification of the Opposites," *Mysterium Coniunctionis*, CW 14, par. 232.
[13] C.G. Jung, "The Father in the Destiny of the Individual," CW 4, par. 744.

"So spoke the child and tried to touch her
father's chin.
But in vain she stretched up her little hands
several times.
Then with a smile her father leaned down
and caressed her,
Saying… Little daughter, you shall have all
you desire."[14]

Artemis asked for many gifts from Zeus, including a bow and arrows, and a saffron skirt. After all, she was going to grow up to become the Goddess of the Hunt. But the most important thing Artemis asked of her father was an "ever enduring *parthenia* [condition of virginity or girlhood]." Kerenyi suggests that this passage from Callimachus's "Hymn to Artemis" "…might just as well refer to some other one among the glorious maiden figures of the Olympian household."[15] It could refer to Athena or to Hestia, who, like Artemis, are also seen and experienced as goddesses of independent women. They too each swore oaths and were granted *parthenia* by Zeus, and thus—even on Mt. Olympus—they were free to become women who were ever-renewing and one-unto-themselves.

I'll never forget the analysand who proudly told me that when she was in college and wanted to learn to drive, her father responded with enthusiasm. He would love to teach her, he said, and he did. And she recalled a wonderful, bonding time while she was taking driving lessons from him. Jung describes the function of the father in a daughter's life

---

[14] See "A Mythological Image of Girlhood," *Facing the Gods*, ed. James Hillman (Irving, Texas: Spring Publications Inc., 1980).
[15] Ibid., 39.

as "…a bridge to the world."[16] This woman's father did indeed function in that way for her. You could see it in the way she confidently walked into a room. "The archetype acts as an amplifier," says Jung, "enhancing beyond measure the effects that proceed from the father…"[17] In the following essays, I will explore examples of the instinctive archetypal Negative Father at work, and of representative daughters, who, when they were growing up—because of the personal limitations, psychological and emotional wounds, and dug-in opinions of their fathers—did not experience "a bridge to the world" in an optimal or auspicious way.

3.

As Jung reminds us, there is sufficient literary and historical evidence to prove that when we are dealing with archetypes, we are dealing with life situations which occur—concretely or symbolically—everywhere, every day.[18] Certainly, in the extensive history of dramatic literature, there are any number of plots and subplots illustrating what we mean when we are talking about the archetypal Negative Father and how it can adversely affect the life of a man's daughter.

---

[16] C.G. Jung, "The Personal and the Collective Unconscious," *Two Essays on Analytical Psychology*, CW 7, par. 206.

[17] C.G. Jung, "The Father in the Destiny of the Individual," CW 4, par. 744.

[18] C.G. Jung, "Archetypes of the Collective Unconscious," *The Archetypes and the Collective Unconscious*, CW 9i, par. 83.

In fifth century BC, the Greek tragedians, Aeschylus and Euripides, each in his own way, dramatized the myth of Agamemnon, the leader of the Greek army, who, to gain the favorable winds he needed for his fleet to embark on the voyage to Troy, was willing to offer up his own daughter Iphigenia to the gods—on an altar. Agamemnon, to go to war, first had to sacrifice the *feminine.*

In Shakespeare's *œuvre* there are notable examples of problematic father/daughter relationships. In *The Tragedy of King Lear*, the father/King actually banishes his youngest child, Cordelia, from his realm, when she refuses to express her love for him in the words which he demands—words she feels are inappropriate. In *The Tragedy of Hamlet,* the Negative Father comes into relief in the character of the Lord Chamberlain, Polonius. *Projecting* his own foolishness and inadequacy onto his daughter, oblivious of the feelings between the two young people, Polonius tells Ophelia that, because she is not a member of the prince's royal class, she must refuse Hamlet's declarations of love. This father's admonishment and interference in his daughter's life not only compound the tragedy but culminate in Ophelia's suicide. Perhaps the quintessential archetypal Positive Father appears in Shakespeare's drama *The Tempest*, where we see Prospero, the monarch of an enchanted island, firmly protect and support his daughter, Miranda, and lovingly guide her towards her future in the real world.

Without necessarily even being aware of it, playwrights, with their particular instincts and insights, often present the archetypal dynamics going on between their characters in remarkable detail. Numerous theatrical works give good examples of men who, in their unconscious way of thinking about and treating their female children, communicate the Negative Father. In two relatively recent American plays, we can find compelling illustrations of how—with the powerful archetypes of Hesiod's pre-Olympian gods behind him—a personal father's mentality, his judgements and opinions, and his human limitations can affect the emotional and psychological development of a daughter—of a woman—in wounding and crippling ways.

I will discuss in depth *A Delicate Balance* by the twentieth-century playwright, Edward Albee. Uncannily, Tobias, the father in this drama, embodies Ouranos. Emotionally absent from his daughter Julia's life from the time she is six until she is in her early thirties, Tobias, in his parental function, fails abjectly to provide his child with "...a bridge to the world." He lets his wife and Julia's mother, Agnes—a silenced Metis, by the way—struggle to play his role, as well as her own.

First, though, I want to talk about *The Heiress* by Ruth and Augustus Goetz. In this play, the father, Dr. Austin Sloper, has it all. He personifies and epitomizes not only the archetypal reactions and attitudes of the pre-Olympian gods, Ouranos and Kronos, but also the destructive aspects of the patriarch, Zeus. With his lack of *eros*, his domineering tone and antagonistic manner, Dr. Sloper keeps his daughter, Catherine, virtually unconscious. We observe the ways he has succeeded in controlling her, and in keeping her small and unprepared for the challenges of her adult life.

"A father's legacy for the daughter is always a spiritual one; that is why fathers have such an enormous responsibility for the spiritual life of their daughters."
- *C.G. Jung*

The Daughter with an Emotionally Hostile Father: *THE HEIRESS* by Ruth and Augustus Goetz

I

First produced in New York City in 1947, *The Heiress,* by Ruth and Augustus Goetz,[19] is a realistic period drama judiciously adapted from Henry James's novel, *Washington Square.*[20] With its great original cast—Wendy Hiller, Basil Rathbone, Peter Cookson, and Patricia Collinge in the four principal roles—and with its strong archetypal motifs, this play stirred up attention in the late 1940's, when it was produced and performed in regional theaters all over the United States. In 1949, the authors adapted it for the four-star film directed by William Wyler, which starred Olivia de

---

[19] All quotations from this play are taken from Ruth and Augustus Goetz, *The Heiress* (New York: Dramatists Play Service, 1975). With book in hand, they are easy to find.
[20] Quotations from the novel are from Henry James, *Washington Square* (New York: Dell Publishing Co., 1962).

Havilland, Ralph Richardson, Montgomery Clift, and Miriam Hopkins. Nominated for the 1950 Academy Award for Best Picture, *The Heiress* received much acclaim and many awards. Olivia de Havilland won the Oscar for Best Actress.

In 1995, there was a revival of *The Heiress* on Broadway, starring Cherry Jones, Philip Bosco, Jon Tenney, and Frances Sternhagen, and directed by Gerald Gutierrez. My personal experience of this production is what started me thinking about this project. When the movie *Washington Square*—based mostly on the James novel but also incorporating ideas from the Goetz adaptation—was released in 1997, it seemed as if a collective interest was generating around the tension between the patriarchy and the *feminine*. This movie version of James's novel, which features Jennifer Jason Leigh, Albert Finney, Ben Chaplin, and Maggie Smith in the principal roles, was directed by Agnes Holland, who gives the plot a contemporary twist in the end.

The Heiress is what we call a well-made play. It is impeccably crafted. Remember that in a play—which usually lasts about two to three hours—everything has to be condensed; events tend to move along quickly. Divided into two acts, there are three scenes in *Act One* and four in *Act Two*. The story is about a wealthy but rather plain young woman in her late twenties who falls in love and becomes engaged to a man of whom her father strongly disapproves. When her father threatens to disinherit her if she goes through with the marriage, the young man, confirming the father's judgment of his character, jilts his betrothed and disappears.

Keeping in mind that *The Heiress,* first produced in 1947, is informed by Henry James's novel published in 1880, I will also be bringing in details from *Washington Square* to deepen our experience and understanding of the play. I will reference the two films which were based on this story, the one with Olivia de Havilland in 1949 and the other with Jennifer Jason Leigh in 1997.

The main thrust of this discussion will be an exploration from a Jungian perspective of what the archetypal constellation of the Negative Father can look like in a daughter's *psyche,* and how it can shape her psychological and emotional development. Where relevant, I'll talk about the tension between Puer and Senex, between Puer and the Negative Mother, and between the Daughter and the Negative Mother. As I interpret this play, examining the characters, relationships, and circumstances in the story of *The Heiress,* we can also review elements of the theoretical fundamentals of Jungian psychology—what we mean by *persona, shadow, anima* and *animus,* and the *Self,* as well as the concept of *projection,* and what we mean by a *complex.*

Now, let's go to the theater. When I saw *The Heiress* in 1996—which, by the way, received the Tony Award for Best Play Revival in 1995—it was a Friday night on Broadway. Although the performance was sold out, I managed to get a last-minute seat in the balcony. The audience waiting for the curtain to rise was very alive. There were a lot of couples and people who had met for dinner after work—had a few drinks perhaps. Electricity was buzzing in the air. During the performance there were ample gasps and groans from the audience, responding to the words and actions on the stage. I'm sure the cast thought they had a great house that night.

The first scenes of a well-made play are called the Exposition. We are introduced to the setting and the time, the characters and the conflict. You cannot have a drama without a conflict—a confrontation between two powerful opposing forces. The entire action of *The Heiress* takes place in the richly and tastefully furnished formal front parlor of Dr. Austin Sloper's elegant townhouse at 16 Washington Square in New York City. Our story begins on an October evening in 1850. Imagine the fashionable clothes of the time: women in tight-fitting bodices, voluminous skirts, and hair ribbons; men in waistcoats, long fitted jackets, and high silk hats.

Using the play to set up a discussion about the constellation of the archetypal Negative Father behind the reactions and attitudes of the personal father in the *psyche* of a daughter, I first need to go into some detail describing the characters and action of *The Heiress*— particularly in the early scenes.

The curtain goes up. *Act One, sc. 1.* The action begins. We see a young parlor maid, Maria, lighting an ornate kerosene lamp. We hear the sound of a carriage passing in the street outside: Clip, clop . . . clip clop. The sound of a carriage passing on the street outside becomes a significant sound effect in this drama, as we shall find out later. We hear the front door open and close. The distinguished Dr. Austin Sloper, a man in his fifties, his successful physician *persona* in place, arrives home from work. It seems he is late this evening; he has just delivered a baby boy in the neighborhood. We observe a ritual of entrance: The parlor maid takes his coat and top hat, brings him sherry and biscuits, and they have a brief, pleasant chat.

Dr. Sloper says to the maid, "Maria, when you are married, you must have a lot of children. That way you won't put all your hopes on one. Give yourself more than a single chance." He asks the whereabouts of his daughter, Catherine. Already, during the very first moments of the play, we get a critical piece of information: Dr. Sloper is disappointed in his only child.

The next person to enter the scene is the doctor's recently widowed sister, Lavinia Penniman. In the stage directions she is described as *A middle-aged lady in somewhat coquettish mourning.* Imagine black lace and bangles and black velvet hair ribbons. Mrs. Penniman has recently come to New York City from Poughkeepsie to pay a visit to her brother and to her niece, Catherine. It appears the doctor is having a small gathering at his home later that evening in honor of the engagement and imminent marriage of his young niece, Marian, the daughter of his other sister, Elizabeth Almond.

Dr. Sloper discusses plans for the reception with Lavinia. Then he asks her if she would be willing to stay with them in the city for several months to be a companion to Catherine when he goes to a medical conference in Paris in December. Lavinia is most happy to oblige. We learn a little more about the way this father thinks about his daughter. We hear from him that when he has guests, Catherine usually hides in the pantry. He says, "Help her to be clever, Lavinia. I should so like her to be a clever woman." Mrs. Penniman answers, "But she is so gentle and good!" As he leaves the room to go into his study, the doctor's tart rejoinder is, "You are good for nothing unless you are clever."

The heiress herself enters the scene next. In a stage direction, Catherine Sloper is described as a *healthy, quiet girl in her late twenties dressed in an over-elaborate, red satin gown with gold trimmings.* In the comfortable exchange that follows between the young woman and her aunt, we learn Catherine is quite knowledgeable about domestic matters, and that she manages her father's household competently. However, from other things she says, we also learn Catherine is shy and not socially adept. She confides to her Aunt Lavinia that she doesn't have self-confidence, and we observe this when, as soon as Dr. Sloper emerges from his study, she starts to behave uncomfortably. It is clear she honors her father and wants to please him, but at the same time she appears unnerved and embarrassed in his presence.

Here is an example of the dynamic between this father and daughter. Catherine has on a new *over-elaborate* party dress in honor of her cousin Marian's engagement. She says to her father, "Do you like my dress?" Dr. Sloper, *eyeing her fully*, says, "Is it possible that this magnificent person is my daughter?" His words are approving, accepting and receiving. His full gaze, however, is critical. Sarcasm drenches his tone. *Catherine doesn't quite know how to take this.* Dr. Sloper continues, "You are sumptuous, opulent. You look as if you had eighty thousand a year."

> Catherine: I thought you would like the color. It is cherry red. My mother used to wear it.

Dr. Sloper: Oh . . . yes. But Catherine, your
mother was dark—she dominated the color.

Catherine fumbles for her embroidery on the chair next
to her. Trying to save the situation, Aunt Lavinia encourages
her niece to tell her father about her interesting day at the
Ladies Hospital Committee, but this only makes things worse.
In a condescending tone, Dr. Sloper replies, "That's fine. I like
women who do things. What is your particular duty to be?"

Catherine: Why, I am to make up lists for
the children's ward.
Dr. Sloper: Well, that's necessary work. *He
indicates her embroidery.* Are you starting
another one of those samplers?
Catherine: Why, yes father, I find it a most
agreeable pastime.
Dr. Sloper: Don't let it turn into a life work,
Catherine.

The dialogue proceeds in this awkward vein until the
evening's guests arrive: Mrs. Elizabeth Almond, the sister
of Dr. Sloper and Mrs. Penniman; Marian Almond, Aunt
Elizabeth's daughter and Catherine's bubbly cousin who is in
her early twenties; and Arthur Townsend, Marian's fiancée—a
quiet, stolid young banker in his late twenties. Unexpectedly,
there is also an uninvited guest, Morris Townsend. It seems he
is a distant cousin. Animated and very handsome, this young
man has just returned to New York City from a European
tour. Arthur brought him along to meet people.

During the introductions and light-hearted repartee, as the family gathers to celebrate cousin Marian's engagement, we watch Catherine going through spasms of nervousness. She clutches at her father's arm. She wrings her hands and crushes her handkerchief into a ball. Until reminded, she forgets to sit down, so the young men have to remain standing. At every opportunity she grabs at her embroidery as if for dear life. At one point she knocks a trinket off a side-table. Her behavior is not meant to be funny. Actually, it is quite painful to watch. It is obvious Catherine is completely undone in front of strangers, perhaps particularly in front of strange young men. Catherine has no *persona*, no face to put on to meet the faces that she meets.

Dr. Sloper is openly impatient and irritated with his daughter. Clearly, she is not behaving like a clever woman. Meanwhile, though, Morris Townsend, the uninvited guest, is behaving like the perfect gentleman. It is his manner that helps Catherine to gradually relax. He compliments her on her handiwork. He is cheerful, gracious, charming. There is something glamorous about Morris. Seductive? He speaks French. In fact, he knows the latest songs from Paris. Cousin Marian and Arthur urge him to play and sing, as he had apparently done for them the previous evening. There is a piano in Dr. Sloper's study. We learn, however, it is a piano that belonged to his deceased wife; it is always kept locked. Mrs. Almond (Aunt Elizabeth) says, "Let them try it, Austin. I haven't heard music here in a long time." Grudgingly, Dr. Sloper hands over the key to the piano, and the young people, with Aunt Lavinia in tow, gayly disappear into Dr. Sloper's study.

Even though he says it wasn't tuned, what we hear sounds like a piano that is in fact in fine tune. If there hasn't been any music in the house for a long time, it seems someone has been coming in regularly to tune the piano. During the ensuing exchange between Dr. Sloper and his sister, we hear music and singing and laughter. While in the foreground, Austin and Elizabeth are having a serious conversation, in Sloper's study the young people and Aunt Lavinia are having a lively good time.

Austin Sloper says to his sister, "Cousin Morris has a royal ease about inviting himself along, hasn't he? Quite the sort of figure to please the ladies." We know right away the doctor does not like this attractive young interloper. And we may start to wonder if this distant cousin, this uninvited guest, is going to cast a spell—or break one. Or both?

From Elizabeth Almond we learn that Morris, who apparently comes from an obscure branch of the Townsend family, did inherit a small fortune, but that he has used it up. Back from his Grand European Tour, he is unemployed and currently living with his widowed sister and her five children. Dr. Sloper, a man of the world, immediately puts the worst reading on the case: "A widow with five children. You mean he lives on her?" Clearly, prejudice has already set in.

The conversation between the doctor and his sister turns to Catherine. Elizabeth accuses her brother of talking about Catherine as if she is an unmarriageable girl, even with her prospect of thirty-thousand a year. Here is a piece of expository dialogue near the end of *Act One, sc. 1*, when Mrs. Almond charges her brother with being detached:

Dr. Sloper: I am interested in every phase of Catherine's life. Detached! Hah, I wish I were.

Mrs. Almond: Why?

Dr. Sloper: Because I wish I could have confidence in her ability to manage herself, and her future with some wisdom, or even some intelligence.

Mrs. Almond: I see that you have none. I imagine that Catherine sees it too.

Dr. Sloper: If you are reproaching me, Liz, you must be more specific. What would you like me to do for her that I have not done? Is there something I have missed? She has gone to the best schools in the city. She has had the finest training I could get her in music and dancing. She has sat here with me evenings on end, and I have tried to make conversation with her, and give her some social adeptness. She has never been constrained in the spending of money, or in the directing of the household. I have given her freedom wherever I could. The result is what you see - an entirely mediocre and defenseless creature with not a shred of poise. What did I do wrong, my dear sister? If you know, I wish you would tell me, for I do not.

Mrs. Almond: I do not mean that you haven't done your duty as a father.

Dr. Sloper: I have been as good a father as it was possible for me to be with the material Providence gave me.

In no uncertain terms Mrs. Almond accuses the doctor of being intolerant and tells him his expectations for Catherine are ridiculously high. Then, at the very end of *Act One, sc. 1*, we get the piece of information which is most crucial for the story that is about to unfold:

> Dr. Sloper: Yes, I expect everything! You remember her mother, Liz. Her mother, who had so much grace and gaiety! Her mother, who was a pleasure to look at and be with! This is her child ... I was entitled to expect that some day she would make it up to me, wasn't I?
> Mrs. Almond: Make what up?
> Dr. Sloper: Her mother's death! She killed her mother in getting born...
> Mrs. Almond: No child could compete with this image you have of her mother. You have idealized that poor dead woman beyond all human recognition.

The first scene of *Act One* ends with the doctor awash in self-pity. As the curtain goes down, in the background we hear piano music, singing and laughter.

In James's novel it is interesting to note the omniscient author tells us that Catherine's mother died two weeks after childbirth. The 1997 movie, *Washington Square*, follows the play. Although I don't really like this movie version, I do find the opening scene, a flashback, very effective. We get to observe the negative archetypal parental constellation as it is happening. In a parlor, we see a cat sitting on a table; we hear a terrible scream; the cat jumps down. We follow the camera up the stairs. We see a man crouched in the corner of a bedroom. We hear the sound of weeping. The broken body of a woman is sprawled on a blood-soaked bed. We see a nurse carrying a wet and bloody newborn baby over to the man. It is the father. He pushes the infant away, gets up and walks disconsolately out of the room. We see the nurse placing the crying baby without even a blanket around her into a bassinet. There is no receiving at the birth of this child, no containing, no holding. No joy.

Helpful to keep in mind is Erich Neumann's axiom: "Every single 'too much' or 'too little' which falls beyond the appropriate range will be experienced as negative by the child."[21] If we can imagine that at birth in the *psyche* of a child there is a space—an emotional need—for a delicate balance between mother and father, of *masculine and feminine,* when Mother is totally absent a vacuum forms. The space which Mother does not fill is invaded by Father.

In *The Heiress,* we meet Catherine Sloper as a young woman. What we see clearly suggests there has been too much Father and not enough Mother. Alas, Dr. Sloper is not only the dominant parental figure in his daughter's life, but he is a father who has been emotionally hostile towards his child from the hour of her birth. At the end of *Act One, sc.1,*

---

[21] "Fear of the Feminine," trans. Irene Gad from Erich Neumann's essay, "Die Angst vor dem Weiblichen," which appears in *Die Angst: Studien aus dem C.G. Institute, Zurich: Vortragszyklus des Winters 1958-1959* (Zurich: Rasher Verlag, 1959). It can be found, ed. by Jeanne Walker, in *Quadrant,* Vol, 19, No.1 (Spring, 1986), 7-30. This essay also appears in *The Fear of the Feminine and Other Essays on Feminine Psychology,* Erich Neumann, trans. Boris Matthews, Esther Doughty, Eugene Rolf, and Michael Cullingworth (Bolingen Series LXI-4) (Princeton, New Jersey: Princeton University Press, 1994).

we learn the doctor has never stopped blaming his daughter for the death of her mother—his beautiful, charming, clever young wife. If this disdain for her perceived inadequacies is what has been reflected back to Catherine day in and day out all her life by her only parent—whom she adores like a god and only wants to please—is it any wonder she has so little self-confidence in social situations, and particularly in front of strange young men who are looking at her?

Like a good, traditional father figure, Dr. Austin Sloper represents many fine qualities: authority and strength of character, logos and law, discipline and structure, goal and focus. The doctor has done all the things of which society approves; he has worked hard in the American way. Although given a head start when he married a woman with money, by his own industry and proud efforts he doubled his wife's inheritance. In the eyes of the collective, Sloper has made a solid, respectable name for himself. The doctor has also done all the right things for his child—and more. He certainly has provided everything for his daughter that money can buy. However, as his sister, Elizabeth, points out, he has done his duty by Catherine without love, without the involvement of his heart.

By the end of *Act One, sc. 1*, we know that in the heroine's birth background there is no mother and too much father. No mother is a Negative Mother, and too much father is a Negative Father. Dr. Sloper embodies a double Negative. He not only represents too much Father, but most significantly he embodies a father without *eros*, without *anima*. As we shall see, he is a man disconnected from his own inner *feminine* aspect.

Let's return to the play! *Act One, sc. 2:* Curtain goes up. Again, we find ourselves in the formal front parlor of Dr. Sloper's elegant townhouse at 16 Washington Square. It is a bright, sunny autumn afternoon two weeks later. Aunt Lavinia Penniman is entertaining Morris Townsend, the recent uninvited guest. Between them the atmosphere is cozy and confidential. Apparently, it is the third time this week Morris has come to call. Unbeknownst to Dr. Sloper, since the evening when he first met her, this young man has been coming to visit Catherine every other day. As the scene opens, he is making it clear to Mrs. Penniman that his intentions are honorable and serious. For her part, Aunt Lavinia is delighted with the company of this lively, attractive fellow, and she is most supportive and encouraging of his designs. She is even a bit giggly.

Lavinia really goes for Morris; she wants good things for him in life. It feels as if, somewhat inappropriately under the circumstances, she is reliving the romance of her own courtship days with the late Reverend Penniman. Or is it perhaps the romantic courtship she never had? In any case, is it possible she isn't paying attention to Catherine's best interests? We may with justification wonder about her sense of propriety—her *boundaries.* She seems to be talking an awful lot about Catherine, whom by this time we know is a reserved and private, self-conscious young woman.

Although Morris appears to be a very nice, good natured, bright young man, he does rather give himself away when he expresses his amazement to Mrs. Penniman that Catherine is not yet married. "It's odd," he says. "In Europe, a girl like that would have been married a long time. Why, in Paris, with her income, she might have got a Count!" Lavinia doesn't pick up on the cynicism behind Morris's words. She finds the thought enchanting. When Catherine returns home from her errand, Morris has just been pumping Lavinia about Dr. Sloper. The stage direction is *pump*. Like a fellow conspirator, Lavinia leaves the two young people alone. And then we see what's been going on. Very convincingly, Morris uses the information he gains from his talks with Mrs. Penniman about Catherine to persuade the young woman he not only understands her, but that he really knows exactly how she feels. For example, when he talks about himself, he is telling Catherine he used to have the same problems as she does around shyness and self-confidence. Catherine can't believe it is possible somebody can understand how she feels.

Catherine is susceptible to understanding. She is susceptible to acceptance. She is especially susceptible to praise. For her, understanding, acceptance and praise are magical. They are transformative! Finding herself mirrored this way in the eyes of such a very attractive young man, a spark is ignited. Clearly, Catherine is overcoming some of her reticence and self-consciousness. The two young people are on the verge of their first kiss when, unexpectedly, Dr. Sloper comes home from work early. He has no idea about what has been recently going on in his front parlor. We have to note here that Catherine has not been sharing anything about her happy afternoons with Morris, any more than *shadowy* Aunt

Lavinia has been keeping her brother up-to-date. Sloper does not know Morris has been coming around every other day for the past two weeks courting his daughter. No one has told him anything, particularly Lavinia—who is thriving on the secrecy and intrigue. It appears that, with the arrival of young Mr. Morris Townsend on the scene, there has been a shift in the family dynamic.

When Dr. Sloper comes in, he sniffs the air. It seems Morris is wearing strong and expensive cologne. The doctor identifies the aroma: "Bay Rum!" A little later he comments about Morris's fine yellow leather gloves. Sloper is observing that this fellow treats himself well. Between the young man and the older one, a Puer-Senex tension is also filling the air.

During the ensuing exchange between the doctor and Morris Townsend in front of Catherine, Morris foolishly betrays that he is not particularly ambitious. He says he is tutoring his nieces and nephews a bit, admitting what he is doing at the moment is hardly a career. "No," he says disingenuously, considering to whom he is speaking, "It won't make my fortune." Incisively, like a bolt of lightning, Dr. Sloper retorts, "Ah, you must not be too bent on a fortune."

After the doctor leaves the young people alone again in the parlor, what happens next feels like Romeo and Juliet on speed. As you recall, in Shakespeare's famous love story, the tragic flaw is haste. But I reminded you earlier that in a play, unlike in a novel, things get condensed and can move along pretty quickly. In James's *Washington Square*, the relationship between Catherine and Morris has more space and can take more time to develop.

On stage, between Catherine and Morris there is now a back-and-forth of "I love you's," and promises of lifelong devotion. And there is kissing. In fairy tales kisses can have the power of breaking a spell and returning an enchanted princess to life, as in "The Sleeping Beauty."[22] Kissing, among other things, is about letting the outside in. Catherine did not experience the intimacy of a mother's kisses. Her father is cold. She never saw her reflection in the eyes of a loving mother, nor was she mirrored back in the eyes of a loving father: I see you. You see me. I kiss you. You kiss me. There can be an exchange of worlds in a look. There can be an exchange of many worlds in a kiss. A transformation?

In *sc. 2* of *Act One,* at the beginning of the dialogue between the heiress and her suitor, Catherine tells Morris deliberately and quite firmly she would never do anything to displease her father—that that would be unthinkable. The manipulative Morris, however, reminds her she is of age and, ironically, with his own ends in view, he tells Catherine that one of the things he likes most about her is her independence. By now we know Catherine is independently wealthy. However, according to the laws of the time, when she marries, her money and her independence will automatically all go to her husband. It is 1850. Of course, her father is aware of the law, and as a father he has a responsibility to protect his daughter. Undoubtedly, he is also thinking about what is going to happen to his hard-earned money.

---

[22] Ad de Vries, *Dictionary of Symbols and Imagery* (Amsterdam: North Holland Publishing Company, 1981), 285.

By the end of *Act One, sc. 2*, when Morris asks Catherine to marry him, naturally her head is turned. She is in love. She says, "Yes!" And she tells Morris not to worry; she will talk to her father that very evening and pave the way. The two of them agree Morris will come the next morning at eleven to officially ask for Catherine's hand. Traditionally, archetypally, it is the hero who tackles the monster in order to rescue the maiden. Remember, Perseus first has to depotentiate the Gorgon Medusa, and then he delivers Andromeda from the sea serpent. But Morris, whose weak *masculinity* is willing to conspire with the Mother figure—Aunt Lavinia—lets the maiden, Catherine, mediate with the Father on his behalf. Morris has felt the doctor's dislike for him, and he is afraid of Sloper. Augusto Vitale, in his essay, "The Archetype of Saturn," puts it aptly: "Puer fears the old man precisely because puer feels in him the hardness and aridity that derive from the old man's lack of contact with *eros,* from the absence of instinct and creative emotion."[23]

In a burst of enthusiasm, the naive and inexperienced Catherine insists she should go first, that she will be able to assure her father of Morris's virtues. Morris suspects the doctor doesn't trust him. He even has the effrontery—totally lost on Catherine—to say he thinks her father might believe he is "mercenary." The word has no meaning for Catherine. In the glow of the feeling of being seen and understood, and in the illusion of being loved for herself, what belongs to her

---

[23] Augusto Vitale, "Saturn: The Transformation of the Father," *Fathers and Mothers: Five Papers on the Archetypal Background of Family Psychology* (Zurich: Spring Publications, 1973), 26-27.

belongs to Morris. For bad or for good, this is the power and the magic of being in love. We see that for Catherine, Morris is like a young god who overcomes her. Her *feminine spirit* is awakened; her sexuality is aroused. By the end of their intense exchange, Morris has gotten this young woman, whom we have just heard say she would never do anything to displease her father, to promise she will stand by him no matter what.

A little later in the scene, after Morris has left, when Catherine forthrightly announces to her father, "I am engaged to be married" and excitedly expresses her passionate feelings for Morris, Dr. Sloper is much taken aback. This he did not expect. Catherine tries to convince him her whole happiness is at stake; he tries to convince her she is exaggerating. Guilelessly, Catherine says to her father, "It is a great wonder to me that Morris has come into my life. I never expected that I would meet a man who would understand me as he has."

> Dr. Sloper: You underestimate your many qualities, my dear. I have always hoped that someday you would meet a fine young man who would match your goodness with his own.
> Catherine: *Smiling.* And here I have found the goodness and everything else!

I think we can suggest Catherine has *projected* all her own goodness onto Morris. Supported by her feelings, and her belief that Morris loves her, she seems to have miraculously lost her reserve:

Catherine: Oh, Father, don't you think he
is the most beautiful man you have ever
seen?
Dr. Sloper: He is very good looking,my
dear. Of course, you would not let a
consideration like that sway you unduly.
Catherine: Oh no! But that is what is so
wonderful to me, that he should have
everything, everything that a woman
could want--and he wants me.

Catherine's outbursts of personal autonomy and initiative, and passionate feeling, are not heard by her father. When she leaves the room, she knows her appeal to him has not been a success, but we can see that Dr. Sloper is quite rattled. Suddenly everything seems to be out of control. For a moment he doesn't appear to know whether he's coming or going; he walks around the parlor with his hat on. But he soon collects himself. Before the curtain falls, Sloper arranges with the servant for a meeting with Morris' sister, Mrs. Montgomery, for ten o'clock the next morning. This is the widowed older sister with five children, who Morris is living with. We are definitely moving right along through the Exposition into the second phase of the drama, which we call the Rising Action.

II

When the curtain goes up on *Act One, sc. 3*, it is ten o'clock the next morning. Aunt Elizabeth Almond has just brought Mrs. Montgomery around to talk to the doctor.

Catherine doesn't know about this visit. We can imagine her upstairs in her room nervously anticipating Morris's eleven o'clock appointment with her father. The aunts—Elizabeth and Lavinia—go out marketing.

From his interview with Mrs. Montgomery, we learn Dr. Sloper is a highly respected physician and obstetrician in New York City, who has also established his own clinic. It turns out Mrs. Montgomery is already acquainted with him; he recently treated one of her offspring. Is it ironic that Dr. Sloper is a much-respected pediatrician? It sounds like he takes good care of other people's children. Sternly, Sloper questions Morris' sister about her younger brother's character. Is he reliable? Is he trustworthy? Is he responsible? Is he selfish? Does he help her out financially? Mrs. Montgomery equivocates; she defends and protects Morris. Apparently, their parents both died when the boy was sixteen, and he came to live with his sister and her family at that time, some fifteen years ago. This is really all the information we have about Morris's background. We don't learn anything more in *Washington Square,* either. That he was sixteen when his father died suggests Morris has an underlying archetypal Negative Father, too. Sixteen is the age when a boy is becoming a man. In the best of circumstances, it's tough to lose a parent, but for a child to suddenly lose both parents at the same time is terrible—at any age. Psychologically and emotionally, when he was an adolescent, Morris lost the ground under his feet and his "bridge to the world" in one fell swoop. We can imagine that—deep down—reality is hard for him to bear.

Mrs. Montgomery says, "I think, doctor, you expect too much of people. If you do, you will always be disappointed." Glancing at a miniature of a beautiful young woman, she assumes it is a picture of Catherine. Knowing Morris is attracted to beauty, it doesn't surprise her that he has fallen in love at first sight with the doctor's daughter. Sloper nicely explains that the miniature his visitor is looking at is not a picture of Catherine, but a likeness of his long-deceased wife. As their conversation unfolds, it appears Mrs. Montgomery does not know about the inheritance. To her surprise, she hears for the first time from Dr. Sloper that Catherine will be a very wealthy woman one day, that she already has ten thousand a year of her own and will receive another twenty thousand when he dies. At this point, Sloper calls for Catherine to come down and meet Morris' sister.

When Catherine enters the scene, she is in a state of nervous anxiety. We would say she was possessed by a *complex*. The whole meeting is terribly difficult. Mrs. Montgomery is kind and patient, but Catherine, bless her heart, has it all backwards. She is petrified Morris' sister isn't going to approve of her, that she isn't going to be considered good enough for him. Even Dr. Sloper is embarrassed. When his daughter leaves the room, he looks at Mrs. Montgomery: "I think his motives are clear . . . pitifully clear. He is in love with her money." Alas, after meeting the shy and clumsy young woman, Mrs. Montgomery cannot honestly deny this is a possibility, but she refuses to say anything:

Dr. Sloper: You see, you still protect him.
Mrs. Montgomery: *Holding her own very*

well. No, it's the girl I protect! Am I to tell
her that she is undesirable—that she is
unloved! Why it would break her heart!
I would not say that to any girl!
Dr. Sloper: What am I to do?
Mrs. Montgomery: I don't know. *Then
deliberately.* But if you are so opposed to
this marriage, then as a father you must
find a kinder way of stopping it. Good day,
doctor.

Now the doctor believes he knows what he needs to know,
his suspicions having been confirmed by Mrs. Montgomery—
mostly by what she didn't say. Actually, in the novel, at the
end of their interview, Morris' sister says, "Don't let her marry
him."

When the two aunts return from their errands, Dr.
Sloper bluntly tells the ladies Morris Townsend is a fortune
hunter and that he is going to forbid the marriage. Of course,
the women are not so sure this is true, or that it is the best
way to go about things. Aunt Elizabeth, filling in the Positive
Mother role, trying to smooth things over, advises a cooling-
off period. Much to the doctor's dismay, she suggests he take
Catherine with him on his trip to Europe later that fall. He
had been planning to take a solitary walk down memory
lane after the medical conference and revisit the sites of his
honeymoon travels.

Punctually, at eleven o'clock, Morris Townsend appears at
16 Washington Square. The meeting between the father and
the prospective son-in-law goes badly. Quite emphatically, the
doctor tells the young man he does not approve of him. "You

have no means, no profession," he says. "You have no visible resources or prospects, and so you're in a category from which not to choose a son-in-law. Particularly not for my daughter, who is a weak young woman with a large fortune." But Morris fights back. He gets assertive. Boldly, he replies, "Catherine loves me." Here we really feel the Puer-Senex tension. As Augusto Vitale in his essay on "The Archetype of Saturn" says, the young man who is a Puer has no form. "When the unavoidable necessity of existence compels puer to take form, the struggle with senex, the negative father begins." The Puer refuses "the bitter cup," which is offered by the father, even though it is the potion which could transform him into a hero.[24]

Dr. Sloper tells Morris to his face that he is a man who has nothing to offer his daughter. However, we have to notice here that Sloper does not offer Morris any bitter cups— any options or conditions. Typically, in fairy tales, the Old King gives three challenges to the young man who wants to marry the princess and become his heir. The doctor only says what Morris is not—not what he could be. Morris lost his father when he was sixteen. Puer needs spirit! Jung has said, "The archetype of spirit...always appears in a situation where insight, understanding, good advice, determination, planning etc. are needed, but cannot be mustered on one's own resources."[25] Sloper isn't offering any "spirit." He does not set any goals or even make suggestions or—for the sake

---

[24] Ibid.
[25] C.G. Jung, "The Phenomenology of Spirit in Fairy Tales," *The Archetypes of the Collective Unconscious*, CW 9i, par. 398.

of his daughter's happiness—give any kind of support to help Morris belong to the category from which a son-in-law could be chosen. An immovable object meets an irresistible force. The two men and what they each represent archetypally are polarized.

By the time Catherine joins Morris and her father, the scene has gotten ugly. The young woman's comeback is, "But he loves me." If she has to give up Morris, she needs a reason. Of course, as Mrs. Montgomery predicted, Dr. Sloper is unable to give Catherine the reason: Morris wants to marry her, not because she is desirable and that he loves her, but because he wants her money. The doctor is only able to say, "You must simply take my word for it." Kronos-like, he is unequivocally telling his daughter she has to believe him because he is her father. Supported by her Romantic conviction that Morris loves her, Catherine loses her timidity. She defies her father, saying she has given Morris her promise and will marry him anyway. This spirited announcement takes the doctor's breath away: "So he forearmed himself by getting a promise like that, did he? *To Morris.* You are beneath contempt." In a snap reaction, he tells them both that from now on he will turn his back on whatever they decide to do. However, Morris is smooth; he is clever. Sensing which way the wind is blowing, he breaks the *tension of opposites.* He says, no, he and Catherine cannot marry without the doctor's approval, that that would bring unhappiness to them all. Finally, they all agree to put off further talk of marriage for six months— Catherine most unwillingly because she knows her heart. The heiress agrees to accompany her father on a European tour.

As the scene ends, Dr. Sloper's expectation is that, when he and his daughter come back to New York in half a year's time, Catherine and Morris will have forgotten all about each other and life at 16 Washington Square will go on as usual. Dr. Sloper's assumption—his position—is that Catherine can't do it. He firmly believes he is in control of her and that she is incapable of defying him. Considering her to be weak and foolish and unable to take care of herself, when the crunch comes, he knows his daughter will not go against his wishes. In the novel he says it over and over again: "I know I am right. I know I am right." With the archetypal Negative Father constellated behind him, for years the doctor's reactions and attitude toward his daughter have been undermining, demeaning, diminishing and devaluing. We have seen how, in her lack of self-confidence and poise, in her social ineptness, Catherine has internalized her father's judgmental and critical voice. It has become the inner voice which tells her she is not good enough, can't do anything right, is incompetent and inadequate—and unattractive. Her father's voice has become the voice of the *negative animus*. That is, until Morris enters her life and reflects Catherine back to herself in appealing and positive ways. At the end of *Act One, sc. 3* of *The Heiress*, Dr. Sloper is confident Catherine will never do anything to displease him. Perhaps this man's conviction that he is right is a symptom of his disconnect with *anima*—with his own inner principle of relationship and *eros*.

Like a red thread going back to ancient times, we have the archetypal motif of the father resisting being overtaken by the son or, in this case, the son-in-law. Many a daughter can tell a story about her father's odd behavior when she brought home her first serious boyfriend, or about the sentimental way her father behaved at her wedding. In a father's *psyche,* a son or a son-in-law can represent an impulse for change, a new spirit—a new regime—as well as all kinds of opportunities for continued personal development, including the rejuvenation of the *feminine*—of feeling. However, the archetypal Negative Father does not like change; he wants things to stay the same. His hallmarks are conformity and conservatism, and an unquestioning adherence to collective values. Because he insists on being in control, it is hard for him to let go of anything, whether of power, wealth, reputation, or influence— or all of the above. Thus, the inner forces for psychological change and new consciousness are restricted and repressed.

I will be talking more about this motif as we go along, especially from the point of view of this particular daughter, Catherine, and how she gets caught in the middle of the archetypal polarization of Puer and Senex. But first let's talk about myth. Remember some of the things Jung has said about the usefulness of working with myths. First, "...they explain to the bewildered human being what is going on in the unconscious and why he is being held fast." According to Jung, "...the phenomena of the unconscious can be regarded as more or less spontaneous manifestations of autonomous archetypes...which can mold the destinies of individuals by unconsciously influencing their thinking, feeling, and behavior, even if the influence is not recognized until long afterward."[26]

---

[26] C.G. Jung, "The Dual Mother," *Symbols of Transformation: Two,* CW 5, par. 467.

In the early writings about the Greek gods and goddesses, in the stories by Hesiod, the motif of the Negative Father is introduced when Ouranos starts to prevent his children from being born by keeping them imprisoned in the Mother. The theme develops with Kronos (also known as Saturn), who eats his offspring at birth to keep them captured inside himself, forcing them to live his life and values, and not their own. When in his time Zeus was warned he would be replaced by a powerful son, he turned his wife into something small and swallowed her, so she could not ever conceive a potential rival.

Remember, in the beginning, out of chaos emerged Gaia. It was Gaia, or Mother Earth, who created the mountains and the valleys and the oceans and the sky. Her desire was to be covered by Father Sky as an equal. Every night, Ouranos came down to mate with Gaia, and their joinings were fruitful. Eventually (perhaps he became envious of the fecundity and creativity of Gaia?), Ouranos stopped letting their children be born. Spitefully, he kept them in the dark; he hid them in the cavities of the earth—buried them in the unconscious. Is this where we encounter the beginnings of the age-old struggle between man and woman, *masculine and feminine*—between Power and *eros?* Ouranos vs. Gaia? When the arrangement wasn't working anymore for Gaia, the Earth let forth a terrible groan. In her frustration and anger, Gaia bore iron. Did the woman become bitter and hard? She gave birth to iron. With this iron she formed a sickle. Enlisting the active support of her most recent son, Kronos, she gave it to him and told him what to do. The next time Father Sky came down to lie with Mother Earth, Kronos depotentiated him. Where the phallus of Ouranos fell into the sea, Aphrodite, the Goddess of Love, emerged from the foam, suggesting again that the demise of the Old King brings with it potential for the renewal of the *feminine*—of feeling and new life. In Western culture to this day, the sickle is symbolic of the death of the old god, or the old ways—or of the old year.

Kronos became the first Titan king. He married one of his sisters, the goddess Rhea, and she became his queen. This couple too had fruitful joinings, but as it developed their arrangement did not work out optimally for all concerned either. Fearing he would be overcome the way he overcame his father, as soon as a child from his union with Rhea was born, Kronos ate it. At a certain moment, however, Rhea had enough of this system. Her deeply maternal instincts to nurture and support life took over. The next time she gave birth, instead of handing the baby to Kronos to be eaten, she substituted it with a stone. She presented Kronos with a large stone wrapped in a blanket. Unaware, he ingested that instead. The baby Zeus was hidden away in a distant cave, watched over by his grandmother, Gaia, and raised secretly by nymphs and goats and other animals. The Corybantes, worshipers of Rhea, protected him with their clapping and shouting; the noise of their musical instruments prevented his baby cries from being heard by his father.

When his time came, Zeus gave Kronos an emetic so he would vomit and thus free his brothers and sisters one after the other: Poseidon, Hades, Hera, Demeter, and Hestia. Hestia was the first to be ingested and the last to be liberated. The goddess Hestia was in the Father the longest. With the help of

Poseidon and Hades, Zeus then defeated Kronos. As King of the Olympians, Zeus too was warned he would be overthrown by a son. As Shakespeare put it, "Uneasy lies the head that wears the crown." To assure the permanence of his reign, as soon as his first wife, Metis, became pregnant, he turned her into something small and swallowed her. However, Zeus did have to deal with sibling rivalry, which is also archetypal. To hold on to an uncontested mandate, he first had to fight and win a battle with his relatives, the Titans, and other children of Ouranos. Later he had to put down a conspiracy between his brother, Poseidon, and his sister/wife, Hera, when they tried to gang up on him. After that, for good or for bad, Zeus succeeded in holding on to his position on Mount Olympus until the end of the mythological age.[27]

What does the Negative Father look like in real life? How do the archetypal forces represented by these mythological figures live among us in real human behavior and pain? What does it mean psychologically and emotionally when a father keeps his children out of the light and buried in the hollows of the earth, or when a father eats his children? And what does it mean when a man swallows his wife and doesn't allow potential children, representing psychological and emotional growth and renewal, to be conceived?

In *The Heiress*, Dr. Sloper can be seen to embody as well as illuminate various aspects and degrees of what we mean by the Negative Father archetype. We can identify in this

---

[27] For other interpretations about "Beginnings," see Carl Kerenyi, *The Gods of the Greeks* (Middlesex: Penguin Books Ltd., 1958), 15-22.

dramatic character aspects of the Ouranos Father, the Kronos Father, and the Negative Zeus Father.

I will be talking more about the conflict between the father and the son-in-law in this story—the complicated Puer-Senex dynamic that develops between the doctor and Morris Townsend—but first I want to go more deeply into the tormented relationship between Dr. Sloper and his daughter. If any too much or too little is a negative, with no mother and too much father, Catherine is the child of a Negative Mother and a Negative Father. The archetypal constellation of two negative parents suggests there are powerful forces-against-life at work in the *psyche* of this young woman. Especially when there are two negatives, this can manifest itself in emotional disturbances, personality disorders, and neuroses. In his essay, "The Significance of the Father in the Destiny of the Individual," Jung, agreeing with Freud, says that "...the emotional relationship of a child... particularly to the father, is of decisive significance in regard to the content of any later neurosis." He continues, "This relationship is indeed the infantile channel along which the libido flows back when it encounters any obstacles in later years, thus reactivating the long forgotten psychic contents of childhood."[28] Jung emphasizes the powerful transpersonal aspects of the parents. In other words, there is an archetypal Mother and an archetypal Father who stand, as it were, behind the biological parents, exerting their force and their influence—whether positive or negative—on the development

---

[28] C.G. Jung, *Freud and Psychoanalysis*, CW 4, par. 693.

of the personality of the child. In his essay from which I just quoted, Jung is talking in particular about the damaging effects of an excessively dominating father figure. Catherine's outer father, her concrete biological father, certainly dominates her psychologically. However, he is by no means emotionally absent. He rejects her emotionally every day. As we interpret *The Heiress,* what is important to recognize is that within Catherine's *psyche* the negative pole of the Father archetype was constellated the hour she was born. When Morris Townsend enters the scene, however, he upsets the longstanding family dynamic.

What does the Negative Father look like in Catherine's life? Representing both generic father and archetypal Negative Father, Dr. Sloper stands for and embodies the ascending collective values of the time and culture in which he is living. It is 1850 in upper middle-class New York City in the early Victorian Era. Dr. Sloper is a patriarch; he is a man of authority, power and law. Eminently respectable, he is a successful professional who, in his work ethic, is bound by a sense of duty and responsibility. But, as we have seen in the exposition of this drama, what is particularly worthy of our attention is that this man lacks a real connection to his inner *feminine,* to feeling—*eros.*

Jung has suggested that, to the extent a man becomes social, his personality diminishes: "Psychological insecurity… increases in proportion to social security…"[29] Dr. Sloper is in his fifties. "Whoever carries over into the afternoon the law of

---

[29] C.G. Jung, "Marriage as a Psychological Relationship," *The Development of Personality*, CW 17, par. 343.

the morning," says Jung, "or the natural aim (i.e. the biological or the social aim), must pay for it with damage to his soul..."[30] In other words, we can say the doctor has become dug in, settled; he is not growing anymore—not open to adapting to the changes intrinsic to the later phases of life. Actually, when we first meet him, he is like the Old King in the fairy tales. We have also described Dr. Sloper as conventional and conservative, single-minded and driven. There is no Queen for this Old King. We can say the doctor's relationship with the *feminine* has been ruled by his love for his deceased wife. It is as if his *anima* is out of reach—in the Beyond. When we meet him in the opening scene of the play, the doctor presents himself as a creature of habit, a bit stuffy, stubborn and proud. He could also be described as rigid and unrelated; he certainly has very strong opinions. Dutiful to a fault, he regulates his household with his authoritarian attitudes and reactions; he knows what is right for everybody. We can imagine when his young, beautiful, clever wife died, his own emotional development and potential for psychological and spiritual growth sadly came to a halt. There is no more animation. No more music.

It appears Dr. Sloper never properly grieved his wife's death and still holds much ungrieved grief. In his dealings with his only child, his daughter Catherine, he is not compassionate, much less empathic; rather, he is critical and judgmental. Even though he says he isn't controlling her, he is. He provides her with every freedom, everything money

---

[30] C.G. Jung, "The Stages of Life," *The Structure and Dynamics of the Psyche*, CW 8, par. 787.

can buy, but it is not necessarily what she wants or needs; it is what he wants her to have and how he wants her to have it. As we shall see, the trip to Europe is an example of this kind of paternal generosity. Dr. Sloper intimidates Catherine. We have heard him speak to her with undisguised sarcasm and talk about her possibilities in life with unvarnished skepticism. In Henry James's novel, the doctor actually comes into relief as malicious. He has a more sinister quality in *Washington Square* than he does in the play that was adapted from it. As the omniscient author, James tells us Dr. Austin Sloper, obstetrician and pediatrician, does not like women. Does he—Ouranos-like—resent them for their creativity? In *The Heiress*, Sloper's sister Elizabeth accuses him of being "detached." Particularly as the novel *Washington Square* progresses, we realize more and more just how unrelated Dr. Sloper is towards Catherine and how—Kronos-like—he objectifies his daughter. He stands back like a scientist and observes her as if she is a rat in a maze, watching to see what she will do next and never doubting he is in control of the experiment. His theory is that in the end she will back down from her engagement to Morris Townsend to please him. Is it possible that, unconsciously, this quintessentially patriarchal father does not want to lose the power and control he has over his daughter—and over his money—because this control is what is giving him life?

Since the action of a play has to be condensed, there are a couple of details about Dr. Sloper in the novel that have been omitted in *The Heiress*, but I think they are important to help us get more insight into his history and psychology, because he apparently has none. In *Washington Square,* the story goes that Dr. Sloper and his wife first had a son, but the child died at a very early age. All his knowledge and experience as a doctor could not save the life of his firstborn. Despite all his skills as a doctor, he had to watch helplessly as his wife died two weeks after the birth of their second child, Catherine. Did he become morally distressed because he was a doctor who could not heal his own family? Ever since they died, it was as if a black cloud hovered over him. Was it too much grief? Too little expression of it? First there was the loss of his son and heir, who could have embodied the principle of rebirth in his *psyche.* Then, with the passing of his wife, his personal connection to *anima* and to the principle of *eros* came to a halt. He would not—could not—let it be renewed by the arrival of a baby daughter. Rather the opposite.

When we meet Dr. Sloper, it appears he has never healed nor resolved his grief. There's an implication here not only of the wounding of his *ego* and his pride, but also of the wounding of his instinctual life. He never married again. Where does he go with his human sexuality? All we know about him is that, when he is not absorbed in his profession, he lives in the past. Like Zeus, he has swallowed his wife; he would never have another child. There were to be no future possibilities for the regeneration of his feeling life. Although his wife's piano is in his study and he even has it tuned regularly, he keeps it locked. No one has played this piano since his wife died, not until the young, romantic Morris Townsend—just back from Paris—brings music into the house again and breaks the spell.

In *Washington Square* we read that Catherine was nursed and raised by servants. She never really knew a paradise from which to be expelled. We learn that, growing up, she was a robust child and a welcome guest in the home of her Aunt Elizabeth Almond, where she played with her many cousins. It was in the Almond household where she experienced feeling life. In general, though, in her own elegant home, a heavy and negative atmosphere prevailed. All in all, Catherine knew every material comfort and had all the opportunities of schooling and music lessons and everything money could buy, but something was not right. In the early sequences of the play, she presents herself as a young woman whose authentic personality is suffering from *repression*. Without *ego*-strength, much less a sense of *Self,* when we meet the heiress, she can be described as pathologically shy.

Born into a shaky life situation, Catherine never experienced an optimal primary relationship. Psychologist Mary Ayers, in her book *The Eyes of Shame,* puts it this way: "Eyes are an emotional center of the mother-infant relationship and a pivotal factor in intrapsychic development. The mother's face is the infant's first reflection of her inner self, and it is through her mother's mirroring and responsiveness that the child begins to develop a sense of being and to integrate intense emotions and instincts."[31] Ayers, who quotes Kohut and Winnicott, continues: "This form of object relating, which [can be compared with] primary identification, is an essential precondition for the development of a sense of self

---

[31] Mary Ayers, *Mother-Infant Attachment and Psychoanalysis: The Eyes of Shame* (New York: Brunner-Routledge, 2003), 61.

and promotes an initial sense of existence for the infant."[32] In *The Heiress* and in the 1997 movie, *Washington Square*, Catherine did not have a mother to look at her and see her, to receive and contain and accept her, or to validate and reflect her in loving eyes. Even though she was well taken care of, fed and cleaned and clothed, it was not by her mother. Does a baby know it is not the mother taking care of her? Mary Ayers believes so. Catherine did not experience her personal, biological mother; she only knew the objective mother in the form of maids and servants.

Catherine also did not have a father who looked upon her with loving eyes. He eyed her fully, for example, when she appeared in the cherry red dress in *Act I*, but he eyed her disparagingly and with sarcasm. Nor did she have a father who was considerate of her and respectful. As Jung observed in the 1930's: "...a man's vital energy is focused almost entirely upon his business, so that as a husband [in our story, father] he is glad to have no responsibilities. He gives the complete direction of his family life over to his wife [in our story, his servants]. His real life, his business [in our story, his medical practice] is where the fight is. The lazy part of his life is where his family [his daughter] is."[33]

In this regard, the lazy part of Dr. Sloper's life was mightily augmented by his unloving and judgmental attitude towards his child. In the times in which we are living, there certainly have been changes and shifts in attitudes and reactions

---

[32] Ibid., 64.
[33] *C.G. Jung Speaking: Interviews and Encounters*, eds. William McGuire & R.F. Hull (London: Pan Books, 1980), 39-40.

around the role of the father on every level. Many fathers are definitely more actively involved with their families and in the upbringing and well-being of their children. Jung is talking in the above quotation about the traditional and conventional attitude, which in Western culture goes back to antiquity. In spite of new consciousness, however, this model is still prevalent, partially because of social pressures, but also because of religious beliefs. What is often happening today is that many infants and very young children are deprived early of their mothers in the home as well, not only because more women want to have a career and children, but also because of desperate domestic and economic situations where one income is simply not sufficient for a family to survive.

If Dr. Sloper was inaccessible to his daughter Catherine emotionally, he was not emotionally absent. And he definitely cannot be described as weak. On the contrary! His penetrating masculine presence was felt everywhere in the household. His character, his reputation and his values, his overbearing attitudes and definite opinions dominated Catherine's childhood, adolescence, and young womanhood. As his sister, Lavinia, keenly observes in *Act One, sc.2*, his power to love has withered away. In Jung's essay, "The Significance of the Father in the Destiny of the Individual," he discusses the difficulties of a daughter in relation to her father: "The glossing over of the family problem and the development of the negative of the parental character may take place deep within, unnoticed by anyone, in the form of inhibitions and conflicts which she does not understand. Or, as she grows up, she will come into conflict with the world of actualities..."[34] Socially speaking, this is pretty much Catherine when we first become acquainted with her at the reception for her cousin Marian's engagement.

III

Using *The Heiress* as an example, we have been exploring what it can look like psychologically and emotionally when a father does not let his daughter be born or when he devours her. Now, what does a Positive Father or a good-enough-father look like? I think we agree that he is one who cares about his daughter. Supportive and helpful, he says, "Yes, you can do it!" He provides for her education and encourages her to have an individual point of view. He is a father who fosters and guides his daughter into life and becomes her "...bridge to the world."[35]

Iranian-American author, Azar Nafisi, in her book *The Republic of Imagination,* sums it up very well: "More than anything when I think of [my father] this is what I remember: his sharing of his time and pleasure with me, as if I were his equal, his companion and co-conspirator. There was no moral lesson to be drawn; it was an act of love, but also of respect and trust."[36]

---

[34] C.G. Jung, *Freud and Psychoanalysis*, CW 4, par. 701.
[35] C.G. Jung, "The Personal and the Collective Unconscious," *Two Essays on Analytical Psychology*, CW 7, par. 206.
[36] Azar Nafisi, *The Republic of Imagination: America in Three Books* (New York: Viking, 2014), 7.

Traditionally, it is the father who is the first man in a woman's life. Traveling away from home and coming back again while the child remains safely with her mother, a father represents the world of school and work, of other people and other places. Ideally, commanding due regard and obedience, he stands for authority and discipline. In relation to his occupation or profession, he represents goal, direction—an active and dynamic principle of life. In an optimal father-daughter relationship, the male parent's love for his child supports her psychological and emotional development, and her gradual adjustment and adaptation to the real world. Such a father's active participation in his daughter's upbringing can foster her self-confidence and her *femininity* and, down-the-road, the positive experience of herself as a sexual woman. Most importantly, he awakens her spirit! With his encouragement and support, and his emotional involvement, a girl/a young woman is gradually weaned away from the *participation mystique* with her mother and is better able to move into the world of school and work and, eventually, into the world of her life's tasks and of partnership. As we have seen so far in the story of *The Heiress,* instead of functioning as a "...bridge to the world," Dr. Sloper, with his reactions and attitudes has embodied a daunting obstacle for Catherine both within and without. Like Ouranos, he has blocked her path from Earth to Sky, from *materia* to *spirit*.

To get into life, a daughter needs at least a partial identification with her father and some kind of personal relationship with him. Even though Catherine adores her father—she hero-worships him—however much she tries, she cannot ever really please him. In effect, he always pushes her away and puts her down. She is not perceived by him as beautiful. Her mother was beautiful. Catherine's taste in clothes is ostentatious. Her mother's taste was exquisite. Catherine is retiring and asocial. Her mother was famously charming and outgoing. An *extraverted* mother and an *introverted* daughter?

In the play, there is a revealing exchange between father and daughter after Catherine returns from an appointment with a music teacher:

> Dr. Sloper: And what did he say?
> Catherine: He said the harp was a very difficult instrument.
> Dr. Sloper: Well, we both knew that.
> Catherine: He did not think I was exactly suited to it.
> Dr. Sloper: Why not?
> Catherine: *Timidly.* You need a true ear for a harp. It seems that I have not a very true ear.
> Dr. Sloper: Nonsense—that's impossible. Your mother's ear was impeccable. Why, she used to tune her own piano.
> Catherine: *Looking into her lap.* Yes, father. I know.

Is Dr. Sloper exaggerating when he says his wife tuned her own piano? It was unlikely this was something a lady of her era would do. Even more to the point, piano tuning requires serious physical strength and would be challenging for most women to accomplish in any time period. Remember what Aunt Elizabeth Almond says to Dr. Sloper at the end of the first scene of *Act One:* "You have idealized that poor dead woman beyond all human recognition."

In everyday life, an Ouranos Father is a controlling father who prevents his daughter from being born by keeping her a child—immature, helpless, uncertain, passive, dependent and obedient. He tries to suppress her individuality, her unique *Self.* As we have heard, Dr. Sloper demonstrates no confidence in Catherine's ability to manage her own life. The Ouranos Father simply won't get out of the way.

Catherine can never quite get it right. Instinctively, she reaches for her embroidery; it gives her something to do with her hands and is something she can hide behind. Handiwork, however, can also be a creative outlet; it is an archetypally *feminine* activity. In any case, Catherine's needlepoint is an important element in the story. Henry James, the omniscient author, tells us in the novel that, even though she does a lot of it, she isn't really very good at it. Is it because she has no talent for needlework or because she knows her father despises it? Near the end of the play, with contempt in his voice, Dr. Sloper tells his daughter she embroiders neatly. In other words, embroidery is her one accomplishment, and it is a mediocre one at that. For Catherine, just as she can't seem to please her father no matter how hard she tries, there is also the dreadful thought in the back of her mind that, being as inadequate as she has been made to feel, if her mother were still alive, she would not please her mother either.

When Morris Townsend appears in her life, we can describe Catherine as dependent, passive and obedient. Timid. Probably a little depressed. Certainly, she is unsure of herself socially. It is as if, as a consequence of her mother's absence and her father's overbearing presence, as well as her father's unloving looks and negative attitude towards her, parts of her being—of her unique personality—have been turned to stone. Not to confuse things by mixing myths and metaphors here, but I am deliberately alluding to the deadening effect of the eyes of the Gorgon Medusa. In real life, a daughter can be turned to stone not only by being regarded, judged and criticized by the withered *anima* of her father, but also by the benumbing, dark, and unrelated gaze of her mother's *negative animus*. No mother means a Negative Mother.

To go back to what it looks like archetypally when an Ouranos Father keeps his child out of the light and hidden or buried in the crevasses of the earth, Murray Stein puts it this way: "Ouranos, the sky, defends his position by keeping his young unconscious, mother-bound, encapsulated in dull day-in-day-out *materia.*"[37] In the protection and privacy of her home at 16 Washington Square, Catherine does all right. She is the mistress of her father's household and runs everything according to his particular expectations. She volunteers on the Ladies Hospital Committee, where she has various duties—among them making lists for the children's ward. However, she is also teaching younger women about the differences between cows and calves, and the different cuts of meat. Early in the play there is an exchange with her Aunt Lavinia, where we learn that Catherine—and remember

---

[37] Murray Stein, "The Devouring Father," *Fathers and Mothers: Five Papers on the Archetypal Background of Family Psychology*, ed. Patricia Berry (Zurich: Spring Publications, 1973), 68-69.

we're at the beginning of the Victorian Age here—is definitely not squeamish about animal body parts. The playwright chooses certain details like this to reveal the character. There is an earthiness about Catherine. When she first appears in *Act One, sc.1,* in the stage directions she is described as *a quiet healthy girl.* She is physically healthy, and in her domestic domain she functions well. But notice that even though she is in her late twenties, the playwright calls Catherine a *"girl."*

When we first meet Catherine, it appears she is embedded in what Erich Neumann calls the matriarchal phase of *feminine* development, unable to stand on her own two feet in vital areas of the real world.[38] She has too little positive forward-urging *animus.* She was never exposed to her mother's *positive animus* either—her mother's *feminine spirit.* Yes, she is a volunteer at the hospital, but probably as her father-the-doctor's daughter. At home she is uncomfortable in the drawing room, her mother's sphere, but she does feel comfortable in the pantry or in the kitchen—preparing things for the enjoyment of others. By blocking her access to spirit with his unloving and unreceiving eyes and manner, Dr. Sloper's influence has had a retarding effect on the psychological and emotional development of his daughter. By implying she can't do anything right in her own right, he is keeping her down, anonymous, and in the background. With his impatience and distaste, he is virtually standing in the way of Catherine's emergence into life and the world.

---

[38] Erich Neumann, "Fear of the Feminine," trans. by Irene Gad from "Die Angst," *Studien aus dem C.G. Jung Institute, Zurich, Vortragszyklus des Winters,* 1958-1959. Appears in *Quadrant,* Vol.19, No. 1, Spring, 1986.

Unconsciously perhaps, he is keeping her in her place. Keeping her in the kitchen? The kitchen is considered a very important room in a house. Traditionally, it is the woman's domain—the territory of the Mother. Symbolically, the kitchen represents the emotional center of a home. There is a hearth or a stove in the kitchen. It is a positive place of warmth and nurturing, and it can also be a place for innovation and creativity. Most importantly, the kitchen can be seen and understood as a vessel of transformation. In this case, however, I do not mean the positive kitchen. We have seen that any too much or too little is a negative. Concretely, historically, for many women the kitchen has also been known to be connected with pure drudgery and—not infrequently—with death by fire. It is an area where a woman can in fact find herself, as Murray Stein put it, "encapsulated in dull day-in-day-out *materia.*" Here is a good place to introduce the goddess Hestia into our discussion.

In her provocative essay, "Hestia, Goddess of the Hearth," Stephanie A. Demetrakopoulos reminds us that of the Olympian gods, Hestia was the first one to be swallowed by Kronos. After defeating his father, as king of the Olympians, Zeus liberated his siblings: Poseidon, Hades, Hera, Demeter, and Hestia. Hestia was the last one to be freed.[39] Even though she is the one who is the most anonymous, the one who is always in the background, we know Hestia is very important; she is the Goddess of Hearth Keeping, of Home Making and Housekeeping. She is the one who sits by the fire at the center of

---

[39] Stephanie A. Demetrakopoulos, "Hestia: Goddess of the Hearth," *Spring,* 1979, 70-71.

the home, ever present for the needs of others—ever receiving. However, the extreme of Hestia or of a Hestia woman, would be someone who sacrifices her whole identity to supporting the life systems of others, what Demetrakopoulos calls, "a sort of monomaniacal Hestia." Since Hestia was the first one to be swallowed by Kronos, she is the one who lived in the Father the longest. Demetrakopoulos warns of the danger of a woman being swallowed by the Hestia archetype—in other words, by becoming *obsessive-compulsive* about housekeeping—driven, one-sided and single-minded about it. Could we say *animus possessed* about it? That can happen when homemaking becomes automatic and mechanical, when there is no longer real heart in the hearth-keeping.

Sometimes it is possible to recognize Hestia as a *shadow* aspect of an analyst, who in a positive way holds the hot center of the sacred vessel of transformation, supporting healing and redemption, and the unfolding of the personalities of others in a process of inner housekeeping. Serving as this vessel, however, can eventually become a negative place for an analyst, who, while attending to the healing of others, neglects his or her own personal development and creativity, and gets burned-out.

In general, as long as a woman remains in the domestic or the maternal sphere, she does not violate her nature. To quote Neumann again from his essay, "The Fear of the Feminine": "In so far as she stays within this enclosure, she is to be sure childish and immature from the point of view of conscious development, but she is not estranged from herself." We have seen that Catherine Sloper, who is ill at ease in the drawing room, feels safe in the kitchen and the pantry. Not having had a personal mother, she finds comfort in the archetypal world of Mother, where she does what, to all appearances, she is quite good at. In the big picture, on the path of the psychological development of the *feminine*, we can say that in order to become a whole person and fully human, a woman needs to reach out beyond that safe place—as Neumann has so eloquently put it when he said the evolution from Mother to Father archetype is absolutely essential for both sexes.

Jung tells us, "A father's legacy for the daughter is always a spiritual one; that is why fathers have such an enormous responsibility for the spiritual life of their daughters."[40]

By blocking his daughter's emergence into life and the greater world, by blocking her active spirit—the spirit of curiosity, the spirit of adventure, the spirit of discovery—the Ouranos Father fails her. This is also where the Kronos Father fails, when he holds his daughter's spirit captive inside himself.

To move on from the Ouranos Father, who does not let his daughter be born but tries to keep her in the dark, unconscious in the cavities of the earth—or in the kitchen, or in the bedroom, or in the church—what does it look like when a Kronos Father devours his daughter? In all kinds of ways, a Kronos Father tries to possess her and keep her in his power. Ultimately, he tries to deny her her *Self*—the development of her unique personality and individual human possibilities.

---

[40] C.G. Jung, *Children's Dreams*, ed. Lorenz Jung with Maria Meyer-Grass, trans. Ernst Falzeder and Tony Woolfson, Philomen Series (Princeton and Oxford: Princeton University Press, 2008), 395.

The Kronos father tells his daughter she can't do what she wants to do but has to do what he wants her to do. When a Kronos father devours his daughter, she becomes absorbed in him. She is identified with him—with his values, interests, tastes, politics. She upholds the limitations or peculiarities of the way he thinks. Wives can also be absorbed the same way in their husbands and in their husbands' lives and careers. The Kronos daughter's spirit is not so much blocked as it is imprisoned. Her original personality, her *femininity*, her spontaneity and individual point of view, her personal gifts and enthusiasms are all held hostage. A daughter's own adventurous spirit of discovery and creativity are trapped in her father's collective attitudes and insistence on conformity. As Murray Stein puts it, "In all its forms the devouring father archetype presses consciousness toward conventionality. [And] consciousness...loses contact with instinctual life."[41]

Sometimes we can recognize the daughter of a Kronos Father in a woman who lives very much in her head. She likes to theorize, rationalize, and relativize. She does not take her personal problems seriously because everyone else has problems too, and other people are much worse off than she is. Often, she doesn't even know how she feels. An analysand in the second half of life dreamed she was sitting in the back seat of her car while her father was in the driver's seat. This image did not give her pause. There was soon another dream in which she was being driven by her father, but this time she leaped out of the backseat in a panic because she realized

[41] See Murray Stein, "The Devouring Father," 72.

he was driving them straight downhill into a lake. Horror-stricken, she watched as the car, with her father in it, slowly sank into the water. At first it was hard for her to accept this was a positive dream, and to understand that the challenge of her *Individuation Process* was beckoning.

Catherine Sloper, however, is not representative of a woman who lives in her head. How can we recognize Catherine as the daughter of a Kronos Father? How is she absorbed in her father? At the age of twenty-eight, she manages the household according to the way her father wants it to be. In the stage directions we are told in some detail that, except for the window dressings, there have been no changes in the furnishings of the house at 16 Washington Square in over thirty years. When Dr. Sloper wants his daughter to play the harp and it turns out she has no talent for the instrument, the implication is that there is something wrong with her. Although Catherine's father claims he has had great expectations for her, she feels guilty because it has ever been impressed upon her that when she does not live up to his standards, she is an inadequate and incompetent person.

When we first meet her, Catherine is a young woman who would not do anything her father disapproved of because, for her, his word represents the word of the law. For example, when in *Act One, sc. 1* there is first mention of the piano in Dr. Sloper's study, she is appalled. The doctor is reluctant to let the young people use it, and Catherine automatically defends him. With a knee-jerk reaction, she cries out, "But that was mother's piano!" Later, she quite definitely tells Morris she would never do anything that met with her father's disapproval—that that would be unthinkable. Is it possible she has been so obedient and self-effacing all her life because she was afraid to lose the only parent she had? Until the moment Morris Townsend invades the Kronos circle—what Erich Neumann calls the Paternal Uroborous—for Catherine to do anything against her father's wishes would have been totally unimaginable. Morris comes in and changes the system.

That the doctor is a Kronos Father is also evident when, at the end of *Act One,* he firmly believes he has his daughter where he wants her and that she is going to bend to his will. In *Washington Square,* he says it again and again: "I know I am right." As a Kronos father, Sloper is certain he has his daughter in his power. He has long forgotten what it could mean for a person like Catherine to feel seen and understood and loved for herself. He cannot foresee, nor can he imagine that what Catherine experiences with Morris Townsend is something magical and transformative.

We have talked about the polarization of the Puer-Senex dynamic as it applies to the encounter between the venerable Dr. Austin Sloper and the young Morris Townsend—the conflict between the father and the son. In our story, it is the clash between the father and potential son-in-law, their *shadowy* connection and the tension of opposites which develops between them. We have been demonstrating how too much Father and not enough Mother can constellate archetypally in the *psyche* of an individual daughter, and how a father, who is emotionally and psychologically dominant, can influence and shape his daughter's life in negative ways.

Before getting back to the play, I'd like to relate a *synchronicity* which occurred in the middle of working on this project. One day, an analysand very excitedly called my attention to an article in an Asheville magazine, *Blue Mountain Living*. It was an interview with a wealthy woman in her late sixties who lived in the area and was recognized as a philanthropist. The title of the article was "Meet Adelaide Key, the Local Heiress Who Doesn't Put on Airs."[42]

The analysand, who presented me with the article, was in her forties. According to a psychiatrist's diagnosis, she was suffering from *social phobia*. In this woman's background, the archetypal family constellation was definitely not in balance. There wasn't enough Mother (a weak mother) and too much Father (a tyrannical father). Her husband, a professional, was very much taken up with his business. It was apparent in her reactions and attitudes that this woman had what we would call a *negative animus*. Always hard on herself, she could never do things well enough to please her inner standard-bearer—the internalized Negative Father voice which always said she couldn't get it right. As a parent, she in turn was hard on her children. Easily critical and judgmental of others, she was opinionated and controlling. She knew what was right!

Recently, she had made a significant breakthrough around her Negative Father issues. An elderly man, her father was socially and politically conservative, and religious. In spite of the fact that he had raised three daughters, he talked like a sexist. He also talked like a racist. And even

---

[42] "At Home with Adelaide Key," *Blue Mountain Living*, Spring Edition, 2005, 36-42.

though my analysand was married and had adult children, her authoritarian Kronos father was still trying to dominate her will and her values—from within as well as without. Her mother, like Metis who was swallowed by Zeus, supported the system with her silence. If my analysand and her father differed about something—politics, for example—in the ensuing argument her father would maneuver her into the old familiar place of youngest child, the good little girl who wants to be loved and included in the family group. He would actually say things like, "If you disagree with me, you are breaking up the family."

In the recent blow-up because of a political disagreement, which was just before I was given the article about Adelaide Key, the father had said in so many words that if his daughter didn't conform to what he expected of her, she was no longer a member of his family. Untypically, this middle-aged woman turned around and walked out of her parents' house. She finally realized she didn't have to take this, and that she had the *ego* strength to break out of the destructive pattern of behavior which had been going on between her and her father her whole life. With newly won consciousness, she was ready to distance herself and prepared to pursue, at a deeper level, the painful process of emotionally and psychologically disentangling herself from the dynamic that had kept her stuck well into her forties.

After this interaction with her father, my analysand was better able to continue her work of becoming more conscious of the different ways his voice, his reactions and attitudes towards her had been internalized and turned against herself, as well as recognizing where they were also expressed and manifested in her own words and behavior to others. By the way, it took about a week for this father to call and tell his daughter he was sorry for what he said and that he loved her. The mother finally came through here.

But why was this woman so excited and eager to share the magazine interview with the local heiress? Adelaide Key was recognized in our area as a benefactor of many worthy projects dealing particularly with health care, and with young people and education. She founded a school for children with learning disabilities and also a wellness center, and in the article, she is described as "the mysterious humanitarian."

Mrs. Key, who raised three children, was left by her husband for a younger woman when she was in her early fifties. Her family of origin had owned the largest newspaper in the state where she was born. After her divorce she moved to Western North Carolina and built herself a magnificent rustic 8,000-square-foot home on a forty-acre piece of property where, except for when she was out doing her philanthropic work, she lived quietly with her yellow lab—practically as a recluse. In the interview, Hestia-like, she emphasized how important solitude and the sanctuary of her home were to her. Touchingly, in the interview, Mrs. Key revealed she felt unloved as a child. In her family very high standards were set for achievement and success. She had had every opportunity in life offered to her, but it sounded like her father's "bridge to the world" was not designed to fit the daughter, as much as it was to suit the expectations of the family. Our local heiress also revealed she was not an outstanding student at school; she did not excel academically. And she had trouble fitting in. She tells us she always struggled with the embarrassment of being overweight. Then she talked about whippings with belts. She said, "That's the way it was back then. I'm not accusing anyone of child abuse." She also said, "The belts and the spankings marked my spirit."

The reason my analysand was so excited to read about the life of this philanthropist was because when she was a child—to discipline her to submit to his wishes—her father had also beaten her with his belt. As a schoolgirl she was accustomed to walking around with red welts on the backs of her legs. Once, the bruises on her legs were so apparent that her teacher asked questions about them. Feeling exposed and ashamed, she pretended she fell out of a tree, but the girl knew the teacher didn't believe her. Today, an educator in a similar situation might ask to speak to the parents, or even make a report to the school counselor intimating the possibility the child was being physically harmed at home. The story of the heiress without airs made such an impression because, although Mrs. Key says in the interview the belts and whippings marked her spirit, it was clear they did not break it. My analysand recognized that her spirit had never been broken by her controlling Kronos father either. Marked, yes. But not broken.

The Kronos father can be found in some dark places. As we have seen, somehow, some way, he will try to possess his daughter and keep her in his power. We can see the evidence that he has succeeded demonstrated in a woman's strong commitment to conventional attitudes or collective opinions, or—for good and for bad—in her ardent association with organizations and institutions. Possibly we can recognize her in the dry intellectuality of a woman who, through her total identification with Father attributes and patriarchal values, has been cut off from her instincts as well as from her *feminine spirit*. I remember a woman who brought me a dream with the image of an egg-shaped head standing on two little feet. There was no body between the head and the feet of the *shadowy* figure. I might add that this middle-aged professional woman only came to see me three times. She knew everything already.

We can see a darker archetypal devouring Kronos father at work in the background of cases involving physical abuse, as we have just seen in the stories of Adelaide Key and my analysand. We can identify a very dark, misogynous Kronos father in sexual abuse, where we also get a glimpse of an aspect of Zeus at work. Zeus, after all, had quite a reputation as a rapist. Perhaps the most insidious manifestation of the Kronos father is in the sexual violation of a daughter by her father—or her stepfather, grandfather, uncle, brother, husband, teacher, neighbor. Whether it is acted out in inappropriate behavior, molestation, incest or rape, it is the penultimate way a father or father figure can attempt to possess and control his daughter and keep her in his power as an object to satisfy his *narcissistic* needs.

You have a child, or a young daughter who is small—a girl with low self-esteem. She is in any case vulnerable, dependent, and perhaps lonely. A father who sexually abuses his child implies many things to her: You have no rights; you are here for my needs and my pleasure; you are nobody; I will kill you if you say anything to your mother. The man simply eats his child alive. Like most tyrants, the Kronos father is only concerned about the way he sees and uses other people. What we mean by being unconscious?

And so, a small child, or a young girl, or a brother's sister—or a husband's wife, or a student or an employee—is isolated, victimized, and rendered dependent and even helpless. Trapped. She will usually be inescapably and forever shaped by this experience. More than marked! Azar Nafisi, the Iranian-American writer, in her *Memoir in Books* entitled *Reading Lolita in Tehran*, talks about the poignant scene in Nabokov's novel where, after her first terrible night in a motel with Humpert, the motherless Lolita comes back to her rapist for comfort because she has nowhere else to go. It was with women college students in Tehran that Nafisi used the grotesque sexual abuse of Lolita by Humpert as a metaphor for the authoritarianism and the suppression of women in their country after the Islamic revolution. Once the patriarch Ayatollah Homani took over, officially and collectively the women of Iran were denied the right to have and live their own lives.[43] In Western language, they were buried alive by Ouranos and devoured by Kronos; they were raped and ZAPPED by the Negative Zeus.

I think we can all agree on the basic principles and noble ideals of democracy. We can agree it is democratic to believe in life, liberty, and the pursuit of happiness—for all. That, whether man or woman, to live one's own individual human

---

[43] Azar Nafisi, *Reading Lolita in Tehran: A Memoir in Books* (New York: Random House, 2003), 44.

life, to express and experience one's own individual *Self* is a birthright—or should be. When a father, who is supposed to function psychologically as "a bridge to the world" for his daughter, denies her that by trying to keep her unconscious, by blocking her, or by locking her into himself—his ideas, his values, his politics, his needs, his body—the individual, emotional and physical development of the child will suffer.

When we meet her in *The Heiress,* Catherine Sloper has certainly not been violated physically or sexually abused. Not concretely. However, she has been wounded in her instincts and in her *feminine spirit.* We have in the character of Dr. Austin Sloper an illustration and an embodiment of what we mean by the different aspects of the archetypal Negative Father, and an example of how *eros* is abused by Power.

In the West today, we do not have an official patriarchal dictatorship that collectively fosters or enforces the suppression of women, as exists in Iran, for example. Certainly not one that is authorized government policy. But as students of Jungian psychology, we are concerned with archetypal patterns and motifs. Remember the archaic beginnings, how Gaia—Mother Earth—created Father Sky as her equal. Remember what happened: first there was the Ouranos Father who would not let his children, male or female, be born out of the earth. Then there was the Kronos Father who devoured his children before they could get even a glimpse of the Sky for themselves. Next came the Negative Zeus, who swallowed his wife to silence her voice, and to ensure that no potential male heirs would be born to threaten his patriarchal Olympian crown.

As we have seen in the poetry of Hesiod, these archetypal constellations are at the root of Western culture and have been active throughout the history of Western civilization. In our times we can say changes are noticeable; major shifts are occurring. But we also know that in the United States there is ever the risk of backlash. It is important to remain aware and vigilant, for deep down Ouranos and Kronos, and the Negative Zeus energies are alive and well. As Jung has said, "There are as many archetypes as there are typical situations in life."[44] In our analytical practices we are regularly confronted with the typical situation of a daughter whose *feminine spirit* is handicapped with *negative animus*/Negative Father issues.

IV

Back to the play! There are four scenes in *Act Two* of *The Heiress*. The setting is the same as for *Act One*. Again, the curtain opens on the drawing room of Dr. Austin Sloper's elegant townhouse. It is a cool April evening, and there's a fire in the grate. Mrs. Lavinia Penniman is entertaining young Morris Townsend at the backgammon table after dinner. We learn that Dr. Sloper and his daughter Catherine are expected home early tomorrow morning, returning from their six-month sojourn abroad. Morris appears confident Catherine has not changed her mind. In fact, he and Mrs. Penniman have cooked up an elaborate elopement scheme, "[A] private

---

[44] C.G. Jung, "The Concept of the Collective Unconscious," CW 9i, par. 99.

marriage in the dead of night." Romantic Lavinia has persuaded Morris—from her own personal experience as a clergyman's wife—that her brother will be appeased, and there will be a reconciliation between father and daughter in the near future. Which is, of course, exactly what our "mercenary" young man wants to believe.

Mrs. Penniman seems to have persuaded Morris that when Dr. Sloper said he would disinherit Catherine if she married Morris against his will, it was a foolish, idle threat. In her support of this attractive young man, Aunt Lavinia is openly and deliberately defying what she knows are the wishes of Catherine's father, and not concerned about the best interests of her niece. Collusion has been brewing between Lavinia and Morris. By this time, feeling safe to drop his *persona* of charming, sensitive and caring fiancé, Morris is quite clear that he expects the whole thirty thousand: "On ten, ma'am, you live like your neighbor. Even Arthur and Marian [the young cousins] will have ten. But thirty is something to look forward to. On thirty you live (*His hand takes in the room*) like this." By this moment in the Rising Action of the play, the audience can have no doubt Morris Townsend is what Dr. Sloper accuses him of being—a cynical fortune hunter. Unselfconsciously revealing the weakness of his character, as he admires the crystal wine glass in his hand, he says to Lavinia, "[Dr. Sloper] has earned this by his work. He believes that every man should do the same. The trouble is that some of us cannot." Morris describes and defines himself as a Puer, a young man without form, will, or spirit, and without a personal self-realizing goal.

As for Aunt Lavinia Penniman, in James's novel it is brought into relief more sharply and critically than it is in the Goetz's play—that a foolish and immature aspect of this coquettish widow's personality is in love with Morris. In wanting the most and the best for her fantasy son lover, she is as ruthless as he is. In *Washington Square*, Lavinia is portrayed in more detail as a sentimental middle-aged woman with poor *boundaries,* but also as an inveterate intrigant. Her more-than-friendly rapport with Morris, so-called on her niece's behalf, could be described as emotional philandering. Morris, with his selfish ends in view, has to keep making nice to Catherine's aunt even when she gets on his nerves. In the pages of the novel, the *shadowy* Lavinia has the space and the time to get even more irritating for our young man—who is using her—than she does in the play.

In Augusto Vitale's essay on "The Archetype of Saturn," he talks about the age-old alliance of the mother with her son in the struggle against the father. As we have seen, for good and for bad, this goes all the way back to Hesiod—and to Ouranos, Kronos, and Zeus:

> "The mother is bound to puer in an energy-loaded relationship; but the positive or negative value of such relationship depends on how the father constellates. The negative father, the overwhelming test, the threatening opposition of the rival castled in his established power, the hardened parent as a judge - provoke the withdrawal of puer towards the all-understanding mother and her infinite capacity for transformation

as the undifferentiated Great Mother. So puer's drive toward the future is stopped and compelled to reverse its course…"[45]

In other words, in this case, when the Negative Father rises up as an obstacle in the young man's path, the coursing waters of his life recede. Lavinia is not Morris's mother. Still, with their age difference and her personality, and the position she takes in the drama, she certainly falls into the greater field of mother figure, and we can say she constellates the archetypal Great Mother in collaboration with the archetypal Puer.

What would a Positive Mother look like? She would be a woman who is emotionally mature, well-integrated and differentiated, and she would have good *boundaries*. Lavinia Penniman is an enabler; she nurtures and advises Morris to, in effect, remain unconscious, passive and dependent. She does not encourage him, as a Positive Mother would, to have a goal or find a job, or to do what he needs to do to get into a category, as Dr. Sloper put it earlier, from which to choose a son-in-law. Lavinia supports Morris in his feelings of entitlement, and she caters to his *narcissism*. Because he is so special to her, she thinks it's all right for him to live off the fruits of another man's labors with impunity. He deserves it!

Back in the drawing room at 16 Washington Square, the conspirators are sitting together cozily; Morris is drinking brandy and smoking a cigar. The two are settling accounts. It seems Lavinia isn't a very good card player, but Morris grandly

---

[45] See Vitali, "Saturn: The Transformation of the Father," 25.

tells her she doesn't owe him anything; her hospitality this long winter has been his reward. We hear a horse and carriage passing the house on the street outside. Clip, clop . . . clip, clop. The carriage stops. Panic. The travelers have returned sooner than expected. Morris flees downstairs to the kitchen to hide. Where else can he go? Lavinia hurriedly straightens up the appearance of the drawing room. The moment Catherine and her father enter, Dr. Sloper smells a rat. "I detect the delicious aroma of Bay Rum," he says. He notices his brandy decanter is almost empty. He sees a cigar band on the floor in front of the fireplace. "What happened to Mr. Townsend? Has he jumped out of the window?" Lavinia prevaricates, saying he just happened to drop in this evening. Dr. Sloper, the man of the world, replies, "Really, I should have expected him to make this house his club. It is such a comfortable place to rest while other people are working."

There's a lot of scurrying around. Apparently, the doctor has gotten ill on the ship during the return crossing. Maria, the maid, runs upstairs to warm up his rooms. Lavinia goes off to fetch him rum and hot water. Left alone in the parlor, Catherine and her father have a terrible confrontation. By the end of the trip, Dr. Sloper has realized Catherine is not going to give in—she is not going to renounce Morris to please him. Making it quite clear he is thoroughly disgusted with her, he calls Morris a "wastrel." Sloper tells his daughter he has just spent the most futile six months of his life touring Europe with her. Out of frustration and anger, demonstrating once more that he does not see her or have a genuine caring relationship with her, he cruelly says to Catherine, "One cannot give [you] eyes or understanding if [you] have none."

In James's novel there is a scene which takes place high in the Alps where Dr. Sloper and Catherine have a passionate argument. It is effectively captured in the 1997 movie which was based on *Washington Square*. After months of traveling, Catherine finds herself hiking in the mountains with her father. In a lonely, darkening, craggy place, she answers his question: Yes, she still loves Morris, and yes, she will marry him when they get back to New York. With the red sunset glinting demonically in his eyes, as if from a promontory—like Zeus throwing his thunderbolt—in a desperate attempt to keep Catherine in his control, Dr. Sloper curses his only child: "Should you like to be left in such a place as this, to starve?" "What do you mean?" cries the young woman. "That will be your fate—that's how he will leave you." In the growing twilight, from where Catherine is standing, it looks like a very barren place. Power is working hard here to crush *eros*. Could the desolation Sloper is pointing out be a *projection* of his own bitter inner landscape?

Theoretically, by taking his daughter on an extended tour of Europe in the early 1850's, a father indeed appears to be performing his function as a "bridge to the world." He is showing his daughter "the world." Catherine gets royally exposed to history and culture, to art and fashion—to all of it. When she comes back, the first thing Lavinia notices is how "French" she looks. Dr. Sloper, however, in his Kronos Father aspect, has taken his daughter to Europe as a tool to serve his own ends. The trip was not really for the benefit of

Catherine's education and personal development, as much as it was a manipulative power play to get her to surrender to his will. Ironically, when he has her in "the world," it is his world, the world of his memories and fantasies. When she doesn't share it, or experience it the way he wants her to, when she is clearly not giving in to his wishes, he becomes like Zeus thundering on Olympus: ZAP! His lightning flashes. He strikes her down. At this point in the novel, still unwilling to accept that his daughter will not give Morris up to please him, Dr. Sloper forces Catherine to travel with him for yet another six months—to no avail. She does not change her mind. She will stay true to Morris. As she says later in the play, "Morris is the only one! I have never heard tenderness in anyone's voice but his!" How sad for Catherine.

Back to the parlor at 16 Washington Square. On the evening of their return from Europe, there is this painful, devastating exchange between father and daughter, which leads up to the Climax of the play and the brutal betrayal of *eros* by the forces against life:

> Dr. Sloper: [Morris] ought to be very thankful to me; I've done a mighty good thing for him in taking you abroad. *His ironic inflection increases.* Six months ago you were perhaps a little limited —a little rustic: but now you have everything! You have seen everything and appreciated everything. You will be a most entertaining companion.
> Catherine: I will try to be.
> Dr. Sloper: You will have to be very witty indeed, my dear girl! Your gaiety and

brilliance will have to make up the difference between the ten thousand a year you will have and the thirty thousand he expects.

Catherine: He does not love me for that.

Dr. Sloper: *Slowly and with contempt.* No? What else, then, Catherine? Your beauty? Your grace? Your charm? Your quick tongue and subtle wit?

Catherine: He admires me.

Dr. Sloper: Catherine, I've been reasonable with you. I've tried not to be unkind, but now it's time for you to realize the truth. How many women and girls do you think he might have had in this town?

Catherine: He finds me—pleasing.

Dr. Sloper: Yes, I'm sure he does. A hundred are prettier, and a thousand more clever, but you have one virtue that outshines them all!

Catherine: *Fearfully.* What—what is that?

Dr. Sloper: Your money.

Catherine: *Puts her face in her hands.* Oh, Father! What a monstrous thing to say to me....!

Dr. Sloper: I don't expect you to believe that. I've known you all your life and have yet to see you learn anything. *He rises and sees her embroidery frame.* With one exception, my dear...you embroider neatly. *He picks up his glass.* Well, since I shan't be at your wedding, I'll drink your health up in my bed...Good night, daughter mine! *He goes upstairs. Catherine, crushed, remains seated, her head bowed.*

ZAP ZAP ZAP. Remember Mrs. Montgomery's words? Remember Morris' sister's more *feminine* standpoint? She says, "If you are so opposed to this marriage, Doctor, then as a father you must find a kinder way of stopping it." Ultimately, Dr. Sloper does exactly what Mrs. Montgomery said he shouldn't do—couldn't do. He tells his daughter that the only value she has as a woman, as a human being, is her inheritance. Since two-thirds of that inheritance consists of his money—which by implication he controls—Sloper credits himself with being in control of his daughter. By controlling his money, he controls Catherine—or so he thinks.

Immediately after this scene, Mrs. Penniman brings Morris Townsend up from the kitchen, and the two young people are joyfully reunited for the first time in six months. Morris eagerly tells Catherine of the elaborate elopement plan. Catherine, however, won't wait until tomorrow. She will not be controlled by her father anymore. Taking her life into her own hands, taking charge of her life for the first time, she persuades her betrothed that they have to run away together this very night. Totally trusting him, Catherine tells Morris she knows now her father despises her, and that is why she will never accept a penny from him. She tells Morris that tonight, for the first time in her life, she has finally understood her father does not love her—that he never cared about her. Guilelessly, she says, "We must be very happy together . . . and you must never despise me, Morris . . . We must be very happy and depend on him for nothing." Needless to say, Morris gets a bit restless. Nevertheless, he promises to be back for her in two hours at twelve-thirty sharp. After he leaves, Catherine—

exalted and ecstatic, looking in the mirror and liking what she sees—runs upstairs to get ready for her elopement.

Act Two, sc. 2: The curtain opens on a stage that is almost dark. Two hours later, packed and ready to leave, and wearing her cloak, Catherine excitedly enters the drawing room. We hear a horse and carriage in the street outside. *Clip, clop . . . clip, clop.* She rushes to the window. The carriage passes by. Alas, the ever-meddlesome Aunt Lavinia appears carrying a candle. When she learns of the new plan, it is too exciting. She wants to go with the eloping couple. There is the sound of another carriage passing. When Catherine tells her aunt that she and Morris will not accept the inheritance from her father, Lavinia is appalled and incredulous: "Oh, Catherine, even if you felt as you did about your father, why did you tell Morris *now?*" We can call Catherine guileless, but I think it's more to the point to describe her as a straight shooter. "Why, I had to tell him now," she replies. "He is to be my husband." "You should have waited," answers the *shadowy* Lavinia. "You should have waited until you were married!" Mrs. Penniman, the clergyman's widow, realizes Catherine's honesty to her betrothed has frustrated and thwarted her own personal scheme for Morris. It is after all Lavinia's firm opinion that Dr. Sloper will relent in the end. Now she believes Catherine has not only ruined her chance for marriage but, more saliently for Lavinia, Morris's opportunity to become a wealthy man.

We hear the sound of another carriage on the street outside. *Clip, clop . . . Clip, clop.* "There he is," cries Catherine, but the carriage keeps going. It does not stop. A church bell rings. By this time, it is twelve forty-five. Another carriage passes. Lavinia gives away her part in this drama when she tells her niece it was a terrible mistake for her to share with Morris that she was never going to accept her inheritance from her father. Catherine, after all, cannot compare herself to her cousin, Marian, who, with her ten-thousand, was a beauty and a belle. Catherine bursts out: "You think what my father thinks! You think I am dull and ugly! Well, you are wrong! Morris loves me! *As if quoting.* I am everything he ever yearned for in a woman."

But Morris doesn't come. Before you know it, the clock strikes one. Finally, reality dawns. Catherine cries out hysterically, "He must take me away. He must love me. No one can live without love. You can't bear it in the end... Someone must love me, someone must tell me he wants me! I have never had anyone!" *She tears off her cloak which falls on the floor.* The young woman cannot protect herself from the truth any longer. In the darkness of the drawing room, the truth is blindingly clear. Morris is not coming to fetch her for a midnight elopement. She has been jilted. "I used to think my misfortune was that mother died," she cries, unwilling to be comforted. "But I don't think so anymore. She was so clever, that if she had lived, she too could not have loved me." Feeling totally exposed and vulnerable, Catherine succumbs emotionally to a sense of utter shame and mortification.

As a lifelong devotee of live theater, what happened next on the stage that Friday night on Broadway, I count among the most memorable moments I have experienced watching a performance. Cherry Jones, the actress who played *The Heiress,* was inspired: Overwhelmed by the awful realization that Morris has rejected her and believing that in her whole life no one has ever loved her for herself, Catherine sinks to her knees. With the great hoop of her dress encircling her as she slowly descends to the floor, the abundant fabric of her voluminous skirt rose around her and engulfed her. It was as if the earth had opened up and swallowed Catherine. The visual impact of this tableau was stunning. It was as if Catherine was being buried alive in *materia*.

In her study, *The Eyes of Shame*, psychologist Mary Ayers, (discussing the views of Wurmser) says, "Shame anxiety is the fear of total object loss and self-loss."

> "...every instance of shame is a time of painful incapacity, an endless moment when one is overcome with the existential feelings of defeat and unlovability. There is a momentary, fleeting kind of shame in the normal range of human experience that will affect everyone to some degree throughout the life cycle as an inevitable part of growing up. This kind of shame is easily overcome. With some individuals, however, these feelings may conceal some deeper aspect of shame. A fundamental notion involving the whole self that one is in some way defective and unlovable down to the core of one's being. An individual burdened with this type of shame goes far beyond the normal everyday kind of shame with which anyone can readily relate; one stops being a human being and is petrified by the movements of life. Early infancy is the place where this type of shame develops..."[46]

---

[46] See Ayers, *Mother-Infant Attachment and Psychoanalysis*, 10-11.

For our story, I find it relevant in this discussion that Mary Ayers links the origins of the petrifying function of shame to a disturbance in the baby's eye contact with the mother in the first days of life. If no mother is a Negative Mother, we could say that no early eye contact with the birth mother is like receiving the terrifying Medusa stare. Remember that in *The Heiress* and in the 1997 movie version of *Washington Square*, Catherine's mother died in childbirth. Catherine never experienced receiving, containing and holding, or a loving mirroring of her reflection in her mother's eyes.

Nor was she reflected back to herself in the loving eyes of a father. In lieu of her father, it is Morris who becomes her "bridge to the world." When he rejects and abandons her, all of Catherine's primary wounds become brutally re-traumatized. She falls into the abyss. In this drama, we have an illustration of how experiencing the archetypal Negative Father "molds" the destiny of the daughter. Even though Dr. Sloper says he wants Catherine to be a clever woman, all her life she has received little more than criticism and judgment from him; she has only heard about her shortcomings. Psychologically and emotionally the voice of the Negative Father has been constellated in her psyche, the voice of the *negative animus*. Morris played her mother's piano, which suggests he also awakened the feeling of motherlove in her psyche. If he did, it was short-lived. When Morris jilts Catherine, it is as if all the unflattering things her father ever told her about herself have been validated and affirmed. Every autonomous complex is detonated. Confronted with the huge obstacle in her path of Morris's rejection, all of the inner father's unaccepting reactions and attitudes turn Catherine against herself.

To go back to Jung's words: "The emotional relationship of a child . . . particularly to the father, is of decisive significance in regard to the content of any later neurosis. This relationship is indeed the infantile channel along which the libido flows back when it encounters any obstacles in later years, thus reactivating . . . the psychic contents of childhood . . ."[47] Sadly and ironically, at the moment Catherine is ready to take the plunge into life and human experience in the real world with Morris, her beloved betrays her. We left Catherine sinking into the gulf of regression. To continue the above passage from Jung's essay, "The Significance of the Father in the Life of the Individual": "It is ever so in life, when we draw back before too great an obstacle, say the threat of some severe disappointment or the risk of some far-reaching decision. The energy stored up for the solution of the task flows back and the old river-beds, the obstacle systems of the past, are filled up again."

Back to the play. *Act Two, sc. 3. A rainy morning three days later.* We learn from Aunt Lavinia that her niece has remained in her room for three days and hasn't eaten or slept. When Catherine finally comes downstairs again, she looks through the mail furtively. For the moment, the blinding pain and shock of Morris's betrayal somewhat in abeyance, she is now in *denial* and into magical thinking. That he hasn't communicated with her in any shape or form must mean he

---

[47] C.G. Jung, "The Father in the Destiny of the Individual," CW 4, par. 693.

is ill? Perhaps Morris needs her! Dr. Sloper appears. He has been unwell and has also been staying in his room. He comes downstairs now because—driven as usual—much against the wishes of Lavinia and Maria, he insists on making a house-call. He notices Catherine is looking feverish. She has not been to see him. Concluding his daughter has given Morris up after all, with as much self-satisfaction as he can muster given his weakened condition, believing she has finally surrendered to his will and that he has won the battle in the end, he tells his daughter he is very proud of her. Distracted, unable to speak to the absurdity of his observation, she leaves the room.

The doorbell rings. It is cousin Marian dropping by to welcome the travelers home. On his way out, after hearing the good tidings that his niece is pregnant, Dr. Sloper asks Marian to be kind to Catherine and to visit her often. Catherine, hearing the name Townsend and thinking it is Morris, dashes back into the drawing room. Hiding her disappointment as best she can under the circumstances, she graciously receives her cousin and friend, who is now, after all, Mrs. Townsend. Remember, Morris is a distant cousin of Marian's husband, Arthur Townsend. From Marian, who does not know about what happened between Catherine and Morris, we learn Morris has recently borrowed money from Arthur to travel to California, and that he left the night before to join the gold rush. Taking in the full implication of this news, Catherine says, *With first show of strength.* "He will go to great lengths to find it."

There follows a touching scene between the two young women. Catherine tells her cousin she has baby clothes for her that she got in Paris. Marian says, "That was wonderfully thoughtful. Mother must have written you."

> Catherine: *After a pause.* I want you to have everything.
> Marian: Catherine, dear! Of course, there is nothing you could have brought me that I would appreciate more!
> Catherine: Would you like to see the baby things? 1 have them unpacked…They are in my room.
> Maria: Oh, I'd love to Cathie! I will take very good care of everything. And someday I will give them all back to you.
> Catherine: No; I will never need them.

The two young women go upstairs together to look at the baby clothes. This scene is especially poignant because Catherine did not know Marian was pregnant. She bought the beautiful baby clothes in Paris for herself—for the babies she was going to have with Morris. Of course, Marian has no idea. And from this exchange between the cousins, we can imagine some of what was going on up in Catherine's room during the three days she secluded herself, not seeing anyone, not eating or sleeping. We can imagine she unpacked the baby clothes and looked at them brokenheartedly for a long time. When Catherine gives away the baby things to her cousin, saying, "I will never need them," it is as if, after learning Morris has left New York for California without saying a word to her, she knows there can be no more *denial* of the truth of her beloved's betrayal. But she is also saying "No!" to her future. She is saying "No!" to any future possibilities of being a married woman and a mother. She is saying "No!" to herself as a biological and a sexual woman.

When Dr. Sloper returns from his call, it is clear he is unwell. It seems that on the way to see his patient, he almost fainted. Examining himself with the new medical instrument he bought in Paris—a stethoscope—he tells the women he is seriously ill, that his lungs are affected, and he is not going to recover. Sternly, he instructs them how to manage his sick room. There is a final scene between Catherine and her father. When she tells him the truth that Morris jilted her, the doctor tries to be sympathetic. But he also tries to get her to admit he was right, that he was right all along in wanting to protect her from Morris. Catherine says, "No." Bitterly, she says, "You thought any handsome, clever man would be as bored with me as you were. And would love me as little as you did. It was not love that made you protect me. It was contempt. Am I to thank you for that?" She then says to her father, "You cheated me."

> Dr. Sloper: Better to know now than twenty years hence.
> Catherine: Why? I lived with you for twenty years before I found out that you didn't love me. I don't know that Morris would have hurt me or starved me for affection more than you did.
> Dr. Sloper: You have found a tongue at last, Catherine. Is it only to say such terrible things to me?
> Catherine: Yes. This is a field where you will not compare me to my mother.

Dr. Sloper can't leave it alone. He tries to make his daughter promise she will not pursue Morris with her money. Catherine refuses to make such a promise. She dares her father to change his will and says she doesn't care. When he tells her he is dying, she taunts him, saying then he will never know, will he?

At the end of *Act Two, sc. 3*, we also do not know whether the doctor will change his will. As the lights go down, the last thing we see upstage before the scene is over is Austin Sloper leaning on his daughter's shoulder as they slowly climb the stairs together. Can we imagine that in a strange way, in spite of himself, Dr. Sloper has needed Catherine in order to live? Once this emotionally and psychologically wounded man realizes he does not have his daughter, his only child, in his control any longer, could we say his withered *anima* withers utterly away? His energy subsides. His heart fails—his lungs fail. Kronos-like, with nothing more to feed on emotionally, he has no animation anymore, no aspiration or inspiration. His spirit leaves him. He dies.

V

And now to finish summarizing the action of *The Heiress*. The last part of a well-made play is called the *dénouement*—the winding up and resolution. Here are the stage directions for *Act Two, sc. 4*:

> *A summer evening almost two years later.*
> *The drawing room is the same, except*

*that a large embroidery frame stands near
windows. The room is not swathed for
summer, but the large fern in the fireplace,
and the use of fans by the women, bespeak
the time of year. When curtain rises,
Mrs. Penniman sits on loveseat with her
embroidery hoop, alternately placing her
stitches and fanning herself. She is far
more coquettishly dressed than she has
been previously, although she is still in full
mourning. But her lace cap, her necklace
and bangles, make her a rather dressy
figure.*

The scene's opening exchange is between Lavinia
Penniman and the maid, Maria. In spite of the heat of summer,
this year Catherine Sloper did not want to do what she always
did when her father was alive—spend the summer at a
fashionable seaside resort. This year she preferred remaining
in Washington Square for the season.

Catherine comes downstairs to join her aunt. She would
be about thirty now. *In her large, placid way, she is growing
into a dignified and almost attractive woman. She is dressed
in a filmy, pale dress, a little fussy perhaps, but effective and
handsome. She carries a workbag of wools, needles, etc.* Maria
compliments Catherine on her Paris gown and tells her how
becoming it is on her. Catherine answers *Coldly.* "It is the
coolest dress I could find."

> Maria: It's such a hot night, Miss
> Catherine, I think Cook and I might take a
> breath of air in the Square. Do you mind?
> Catherine: No, of course not.

Maria: Thank you. *About to leave.*
Catherine: And, Maria—you are as free
in this house as I. When you want a small
favor, you need not blandish me with false
compliments.
Maria: *Surprised.* Miss Catherine! I said
what I meant! You do look handsome…
doesn't she, Mrs. Penniman?
Mrs. Penniman: Yes, Maria.
Catherine: We will not discuss it. I know
how I look. *She matches the wool on her
embroidery frame.*

We have noticed before how Catherine likes to keep her hands busy, but also that when she is uncomfortable, she automatically hides in her embroidery. But what has happened to the shy and gentle doctor's daughter? She sounds disagreeable here, severe, ungracious and unrelated. We might say *animusy*?

Still, the final scene of the play opens quietly enough. After Maria leaves, the ladies drink lemonade, embroider, chat a bit. However, things quickly gain in intensity when Lavinia casually drops a bomb. She tells her niece she has seen Morris Townsend, that she ran into him recently at cousin Marian's house. Back from his unsuccessful search for gold in California, he wants to see Catherine. Harshly, firmly, the heiress declares she never wants to see Morris again. When the doorbell rings, she gets furious, for it becomes clear Lavinia has taken the liberty to tell Morris he could come by and visit them this very evening. Now we know why the *shadowy* Mrs. Penniman is so particularly coquettishly dressed up! At first Catherine absolutely refuses to receive him. "You can do what you want with your promise," she snaps. But then, after she hears the man's voice in the hallway talking to her aunt, to our surprise, she relents.

You can imagine it is an awkward meeting. Still handsome but, as Lavinia says, sad-looking, Morris Townsend tries to explain to Catherine why he has come. "Since the night I left," he says, "it has been the desire of my life that we should be reconciled. I could not break up your life with your father. I could not come between the two of you and *rob you of your due.*" Catherine replies, "Morris, my father did not disinherit me. He threatened it, to test *you.*" Here it sounds like Catherine is speaking of her father with some tolerance and understanding. Morris tries to persuade her it was because of his love he disappeared, that he had to be strong for both of them. He says, "…I refused to take advantage of your— feeling for me. You know my dear, no man who really loves a woman could permit her to give up a great inheritance just for him. That is only in story books." With emotion, he strives to convince Catherine he always loved her, that he still loves her and believes she still loves him.

When Catherine, after everything she has gone through, calmly agrees to pick up with Morris where they left off and run away with him that very night, we are totally astonished. The atmosphere in the theater is tense, for the audience cannot believe the heiress is really going to let herself be pulled back into this relationship. Catherine leaves the drawing room to get the ruby cufflinks she bought for him in Paris as a wedding present two years ago. What are we to think? After she goes upstairs, Morris surveys his domain. He is drinking it all in when Mrs. Penniman enters the drawing room. Going to her and embracing her, he says triumphantly, "I am home, really, truly home."

Naturally, Lavinia is ecstatic. She believes in such a love. After Catherine returns and gives Morris the still sparkling but belated wedding present, he rushes off to his sister's to pack a few things. He will be right back, and then the two of them will go to Murray's Hill and tell the Reverend they have been delayed.

Significantly, after Morris leaves, Lavinia says, "Oh, Catherine, we have him back!" Archly, she goes on about Catherine's "beautiful Paris lingerie." She wants to sprinkle it with fresh lavender. However, instead of hurrying upstairs to pack so she will be quite ready when Morris returns—this time to truly elope together—to Mrs. Penniman's surprise and chagrin, Catherine slowly starts to close the windows and draw the curtains. *Then she goes to her embroidery frame and sits down at it. She picks up her needle:*

> Mrs. Penniman: Oh, dear, you haven't time for *that!*
> Catherine: I am working on the "Z."
> Mrs. Penniman: Yes, I know, but don't do it *now!*
> Catherine: *Sewing.* I have only a few more stitches.
> Mrs. Penniman: You will finish it afterwards.
> Catherine: I must finish it *now,* for I shall never do another.
> Mrs. Penniman: That's right! You have better things to do.

Catherine: I have indeed! I can do
anything now!

Lavinia, frantic, tries to press her niece into going upstairs quickly, but Catherine insists her aunt sit down and listen to her. Morris is going to have to wait!

Catherine: "He came back with the same
lies, the same silly phrases. He thought I
was so stupid that I would not detect his
falseness. That means that it is *he* who is
stupid, not I!"
Mrs. Penniman: *Horrified.* No, no,
Catherine! That is not true!
Catherine: He has grown greedier with the
years. The first time he only wanted my
money, now he wants my love, too. Well,
he came to the wrong house, and he came
twice. I shall see that he never comes a
third time.

Stricken, Lavinia moans, "Poor Morris, poor Morris…" In no uncertain terms, Catherine tells her aunt that if she ever hears her so much as mention this man's name again—even in a whisper—it will be a sign she is planning to leave Washington Square forever. Lavinia cries, "Catherine, can you be so cruel?" The young woman replies, "Yes, I can be cruel. I have been taught by masters!"

Unceremoniously, Catherine sends Lavinia up to bed. As she turns out the lights, we hear a carriage passing. *Clip, clop… clip, clop.* It stops! The front doorbell rings loudly. Quietly, Catherine instructs the maid not to answer the door. We hear the sound of knocking, and Morris's voice calling: "Catherine." Nothing happens. We hear louder and louder knocking, and Morris's voice crying out, "Catherine! Catherine!" We watch the heiress. It is as if she is oblivious to the sound. Carrying a small lamp, she slowly climbs the stairs. As the stage darkens and the curtain comes down, once more we hear Morris's voice urgently, desperately calling, "Catherine." The heiress has gotten her revenge.

It is important to make a comparison here between the last scene of the play and the way Henry James finishes the novel. The conclusion of *Washington Square* is not as dramatic as the ending of the play which was adapted from it. Considering the historical periods in which these two works were written and the dominant collective values of their respective times, I believe the differences are significant. In the novel, to get out of the engagement, Morris provokes an argument with his fiancée. Of course, Catherine is totally in love and totally committed. It is as if she has *projected* all her good onto him—all her value. But she cannot pin Morris down. As soon as there is some question about her inheritance of thirty thousand a year, he starts to stall and puts off setting the date for their wedding. Eventually, the young woman gets emotional. She gets clingy. Needy. Morris in turn gets testy. He stirs up a passionate argument between them and, arrogantly refusing to tolerate her impossible behavior, he walks out in a huff and a bang—and simply disappears for seventeen years.

When he comes back, Catherine is in her late thirties. In his early forties, Morris has obviously not done well for himself in the world. His appearance has changed significantly; he has gained weight and is balding. James describes his eyes as "looking strange and hard." Morris is no longer the beautiful young man who appeared at 16 Washington Square on an October evening long ago as the uninvited guest who broke a spell.

As we saw, Dr. Sloper could not be a Positive Zeus father-in-law who, to support his daughter's happiness, would make the effort to guide him to *spirit*. Instead, Sloper was a rigid, unbending Kronos. Everything went wrong for Morris; the inner obstacles on his path were too great. As if doomed to be an eternal Puer, he always opts for the easy way. There is this quote of Jung's, where he is talking about the hero's journey:

> "Whenever some . . . work is to be accomplished, before which a man recoils, doubtful of his strength, his libido streams back to the fountainhead - and that is a dangerous moment when the issue hangs between annihilation and new life. For if the libido gets stuck in the wonderland of his inner world, then for the upper world (the) man is nothing but a shadow, he is already moribund or at least seriously ill."[48]

In the play when we meet Morris again after two years, and in the novel when we meet him again after seventeen years, the way James and the Goetz's describe him, he is definitely moribund, and possibly already seriously "ill"—still looking for the easy way.

---

[48] C.G. Jung, "The Battle for Deliverance from the Mother," *Symbols of Transformation*, CW 5, par. 449.

In *Washington Square,* when he comes back no longer the handsome young man he was as the uninvited guest, Catherine does not accept Morris's explanations for his disappearance, any more than she does in the more contemporary drama. However, it is important to note that in the novel, when she stands up to her father and refuses to make any promises about what she will or will not do with his money after he dies, Dr. Sloper does disinherit Catherine. This time around, however, it appears Morris is prepared to be content with the mere ten thousand he believes she is receiving from her mother. Catherine will have nothing to do with his suggestions of reconciliation, renewed friendship and updated plans for the future. "It is wrong of you (to want that)," she says. "There is no propriety in it—no reason for it...You treated me badly." In the novel, in her last conversation with Morris, Catherine says it two times: "You treated me badly."

When Morris leaves, he is angry; he will certainly never come back. But before he closes the door behind him, there is a brief confrontation between him and Mrs. Penniman in the hallway. Morris accuses Lavinia of leading him on to have false expectations. Even after all these years, he has never really seen—much less admitted—the wrong in his behavior to Catherine, or even considered the emotional and psychological damage of his selfish actions, when he took advantage of her feelings and inexperience of life, and exacerbated all her deepest primary wounds. *Narcissistic* Morris simply cannot understand why Catherine never married; he thinks it has to mean she still loves him. Given the laws and the social status of women at the time, her reply that she had nothing to gain by it is no small thing. The last words of this Victorian novel are, "Catherine, meanwhile in the parlor, picking up her morsel of fancy-work, had seated herself with it again—for life, as it were."

The Heiress is much more open-ended. In the play we do not know whether Morris sees or feels anything, whether he gains some consciousness in all of this or not. However, his frantic knocking and the acute distress in the sound of his voice crying out "Catherine, Catherine!" as the curtain comes down suggest a dawning recognition of a tit-for-tat.

Yes, Catherine gets even. She fools Morris. At the end of the play, we know that out on the doorstep it is Morris this time who is left holding the bag. What happens reminds me of Shakespeare's expression in *Hamlet*: Morris gets "Hoist(ed) with his own petard." In other words, he gets beaten with his own weapons of charm and deception.

I think we can recognize in Catherine's actions at the play's end an acting out of what I call the Medea rage. Even though Jason experiences genuine grief upon seeing his and Medea's young children bloody and dead, murdered by their own mother, he still doesn't get it. At the end of Euripides' tragedy, Jason still does not understand why Medea went to the extremes she did. He just chalks it up to gross and indecent sexual jealousy. He never understands, for example, the seriousness of his ingratitude and of his own hypocritical actions in the betrayal, rejection and abandonment of his wife, who gave him her love and support and saved his life. Perhaps it's an exaggeration and somewhat of a distortion to compare Medea and Catherine. Medea was a strong woman with a powerful sense of *Self* and of her own worth, and in her myth she goes on to become the wife of the King of Athens and to have more children. What is perhaps important for us to consider, though, is the archetypal energy which Medea represents psychologically, and that behind the once "gentle and good" Catherine's deliberate and calculated revenge on Morris, the dark *shadow* of the self-confident goddess Medea was constellated.

Already at the beginning of *Act Two, sc. 4* of the play, we see the *negative animus*/Negative Father energy operating in Catherine's *psyche* not only turned in upon herself, but also turned out against her surroundings. We observe this first, for example, in her ungracious and unrelated interactions with Maria, and then in the harsh way she sets limits with her Aunt Lavinia. Finally and crucially, we see it in the mean trick she plays on Morris. We could say Catherine has become hard and bitter, like her father. Cruel. On the other hand, we could also say she has become more mature psychologically, that she has learned how to stand up for herself and protect herself from being manipulated and taken advantage of—from being controlled and used by inferior *masculine* reactions and attitudes. Perhaps at a price to aspects of her *feminine* nature, she has gotten tough. In any case, Catherine is certainly no longer naive. She has lost her innocence and painfully gained greater consciousness. We could say she has integrated *shadow* aspects of her personality—some of her own unlived dark side. Now she too can put on a false face. She too can now manipulate and control a situation with a lie. No longer can Catherine simply be described as "gentle and good," for the dark has been interwoven with the light. She has become a more aware and a more whole person than she was when we first meet her. At the close of the play, we can imagine no one will be given the opportunity to treat this woman badly again.

We can also say Catherine has integrated some *positive animus,* strong and Positive Father aspects from the depths of her personality that are now supportive to her at this turning point in her life. After all, we have to recognize Dr. Sloper also embodied good human qualities. He did have a sense of responsibility for his daughter. The tragedy is that he went to the extremes of Ouranos and Kronos, and Negative Zeus fathering. But he was a steady and reliable man with a strong work ethic. He was self-assured and a shrewd judge of character. These are all qualities which will help Catherine to live with integrity and as best she can with who she is, however wounded she will always be. The possibility is she will never again risk a close relationship with a man.

I had an analysand who, while in graduate school, fell in love with an international student—a man of color. When she told her parents she wanted to marry him, her Kronos father forbade her. He made it clear that if she went through with the plan, he would no longer consider her his daughter. At the time, her mother said, "Don't hurt your father." This client did not stand up to her parents, and she never had an intimate relationship with a man. No one could take the place of her first love. As a retired professional in her seventies, this woman was bitterly grieving her unlived life.

At the very end of Henry James's novel, after Morris's brief and fruitless reappearance seventeen years later, Catherine picks up her embroidery "for life, as it were." It sounds like embroidery "for life" is the fulfillment of a Negative Father curse. Remember, Dr. Sloper sarcastically says in so many words, "Don't let (your embroidery) turn into a life work…" From the novel, though, after the disaster with Morris, we also learn Catherine continues to live a useful life in the domestic area, Hestia-like taking care of her ancestral hearth and home, and that she continues to do good works in the community. Eventually, she becomes a much loved and highly esteemed maiden aunt and confidant, much like what we can imagine Hestia was and wanted to be. Also not unlike Hestia, who was pursued by Apollo and by Poseidon, in the novel we learn—before Catherine slowly and gradually develops into what we today might call an eccentric spinster—she did have two serious proposals of marriage. One was from a widower, who saw she would be good to his motherless children. A *marriage de raison?* The omniscient author, James, tells us the other proposal was from a man of feeling who honestly cared for Catherine, and saw and appreciated the potential of her qualities as a life partner. Apparently, he was deeply disappointed and sorry when she refused him.

The end of the novel feels sad. It was the intention of Henry James to leave Catherine, wounded and alone with her embroidery, in what we would call the early *feminine* stage of psychological development which Erich Neumann describes as "the phase of self-conservation." Catherine had no mother and an unloving father. As we saw, she was blocked by Ouranos, locked in by Kronos, and zapped by Zeus. And then she was betrayed, rejected and abandoned by her beloved

Morris, and totally re-traumatized. Catherine picks up her embroidery "for life as it were." She is stuck there. To use Neumann's words: "[The] unity with and attachment to the feminine coincides with a splitting off from the masculine and a feeling of alienation toward it… Psychologically speaking, the essence of the self-conserving phase is the fact that the dominance of the maternal [or, I would add, the material or a one-sided domesticity] prevents any individual and complete meeting between man and woman."[49]

In the Goetz's dramatic adaptation of the novel, first produced on Broadway in 1947—that is shortly after the Second World War—a subtle shift occurs at the end of the story which suggests a shift in the *collective consciousness* of this more recent period. Catherine does just a few more stitches on her sampler. Significantly, she is finishing the letter "Z." Taking her time and carefully making those last few stitches, she says to her aunt, "I must finish it now, for I shall never do another."

Catherine received many destructive messages from her father. According to his judgement, she could never do anything right or well, she could never learn anything, and was clumsy and inadequate. Embroidery was the only thing she could do, but she did it without distinction; her embroidery was merely "neat." To repeat what she says to her Aunt Lavinia about Morris's fruitless visit: "He came back with the same lies, the same silly phrases… He thought I was so stupid that I would not detect his falseness. That means that it is *he* who is

---

[49] See "Fear of the Feminine," trans. Irene Gad from "Die Angst," *Quadrant*, Vol. 19, No. 1 (Spring, 1986), 7-30.

stupid, not I!" By the end of the play, Catherine has developed self-esteem. She is appalled by the audacity of Morris. When she finishes stitching the letter "Z" on her sampler, she says, "I can do anything now!" We know she has the money, the means and the energy to do whatever that may be for a woman of her time: philanthropy and travel, and the development of constructive and meaningful relationships with family and friends.

When Catherine puts the last stitches on the letter "Z" of her sampler, she has come to the end of the alphabet. We could say she is finishing with a stage of her life. In the 1949 black-and-white movie with Olivia De Havilland and Montgomery Clift, when Catherine makes her last stitch, she takes out a small pair of scissors and carefully cuts the thread. The letter "Z" symbolizes the completion of a cycle and perfection. It can represent an unknown quantity. The lightening-like zig-zag line that makes up this letter could also symbolize the thunder-god, Zeus.[50] When she cuts the thread, is Catherine detaching herself from the damaging power of this god?

By the end of the play Catherine is around thirty years old. She is not only older; she is definitely more mature. When she concretely stands up to Morris, and when with *animus* she mirrors back to him by her actions the way he treated her with such cynicism two years before, it is clear she has begun to connect with a sense of her own worth as a human being and as a woman. Catherine is starting to become—however forever wounded—liberated from the destructive

---

[50] Ad de Vries, *Dictionary of Symbols and Imagery*, 514.

internalized voice of the archetypal Negative Father who, with his cruel verbal and psychological abuse, and lightning ZAPS, has certainly struck her and marked her spirit, but has not broken it. "I can do anything now!" suggests to me again the integration of positive *masculine* qualities. And if Catherine has *positive animus* within, it could be possible to meet it without, whether concretely or symbolically, or spiritually. Perhaps, like Hestia did, Catherine, after the end of the play, will willingly choose a single life rather than risk living under the patriarchal system of her day dependent on a man. The letter "Z" symbolizes an unknown quantity. We don't know.

In the final scene of the most recent adaptation of the story of *The Heiress,* the 1997 movie, *Washington Square,* perhaps to indicate another shift going on in the collective consciousness—where especially in the Western world there definitely are many more opportunities for women— the director of the film has Catherine running a daycare center out of her home for the children of working mothers. Considering the context of the story is the nineteenth century, I feel this ending is unrealistic. You can't forget Catherine is embedded in her class. It is hard for me to imagine her as an entrepreneur going into business for herself, especially in her own home. For those who consider the influence of archetypal patterns set down multi-thousands of years ago, 1850 was only yesterday. Because of the dominant collective values of the greater Victorian era, when domesticity for upper-middle class women was enshrined, the Ouranos Father and the Kronos Father and the Negative Zeus Father all held sway for women, whatever their personal gifts and individual human potential might have been. These gods ruled for women, whose possibilities to actively express their intelligence, individuality and talents in the society in unconventional ways were severely limited. There was no way an unmarried lady could earn a living, except by taking a situation as a private governess. Virginia Woolf sums it up: "There are no professional lives of women in the nineteenth century."[51] We can have different fantasies about what Catherine is going to do after the play is over. With her comfortable financial situation, she certainly has the opportunity to do good things for women and for unloved children, which, I think, is why Agnes Holland, the more contemporary minded director of the 1997 movie—however anachronistically—chose to concretize this at the end of her film.

For the story of Catherine, I prefer the way the Goetz's 1947 dramatic adaptation of James's novel ends. Yes, the play is a more modern interpretation of the material, and it is left open-ended. True to the period in which the story is set, as a woman of her time who has personal autonomy based on her financial independence, I do not think Catherine is going to work for money or for charity. Perhaps she would make an endowment, find appropriate, personal and timely ways— as our local "mysterious humanitarian," Adelaide Key, has done—to support children and education.

Like the letter "Z," the future for Catherine is not clear. We can speculate about what the heiress means when she says, "I can do anything now." Like the letter "Z," it remains an

---

[51] Virginia Woolf, *Three Guineas* (London: Harcourt Brace Jovnovich, 1938), 75.

unknown. The important thing is that—as her father realized before he died—Catherine found her voice at last.

"Where the matriarch or the maternal dominate, a complete meeting between man and woman is impossible."
- *Erich Neumann*

The Daughter with an Emotionally Absent Father: *A DELICATE BALANCE* by Edward Albee

I

"The legacy of a father to his daughter," Jung tells us, is "always a spiritual one, and fathers have an enormous responsibility for the spiritual lives of their daughters."[52] What happens then to a daughter who has an Ouranos father who does not assume this responsibility? I will explore the consequences of an unsuccessful relationship between a daughter and her emotionally absent father as it unfolds between two characters in the contemporary drama, *A Delicate Balance*, by the American playwright Edward

---

[52] C.G. Jung, *Kindertraum Seminar*, Winter 1940-41 (unpublished), 19: "Die Erbschaft des Vater bei der Tochter ist ja immer eine Geistige, deshalb die ungeheure Verantwortung der Vater fur das geistige Leben der Tochter." See also C.G. Jung, *Children's Dreams*, eds. Lorenz Jung and Maria Meyer-Grass, trans. Ernst Falzeder & Tony Woolfson (Olten: Walter-Verlag, 1987).

Albee.[53] By taking a closer look at this play, and particularly at the characters of the daughter, Julia, and of the father, Tobias, but also at the role played by the mother, Agnes, it is possible to illuminate some of the problems analysands present who, during their childhood and adolescence, had distant, indifferent and unavailable fathers. Focusing on the issue of daughters with emotionally absent fathers through the lens of analytical psychology, and using the story of Julia and Tobias, and Agnes, as a paradigm for a more general problem—without, I hope, forcing or distorting the playwright's overall intentions—I am going to bring into relief what I feel demonstrates a moment of transition and possibly the beginning of a process of transformation in the psychological and emotional development of Julia. It is a moment which takes place in the course of the action of this play in a long overdue confrontation between a father and daughter who have been estranged for many years.

II

A Delicate Balance opened on Broadway in 1966. Directed by Alan Schneider and featuring Jessica Tandy, Hume Cronyn, and Marian Seldes, the play received the Pulitzer Prize for drama the following year. Adapted for the screen by

---

[53] All quotations from this play are taken from Edward Albee, *A Delicate Balance* (New York: Pocket Books, Inc., 1967). Page references have been omitted. With the play in hand, the quotations are easy to find. Characteristically, Albee keeps adding background information throughout the play which, in the structure of the more traditional "well-made-play," would be found in the exposition or first act.

Albee, The American Film Theatre produced it in 1973. It was directed by Tony Richardson and starred Katharine Hepburn, Paul Scofield, and Lee Remick.

The setting, which is the same throughout the play, is the living room of a luxurious suburban home. The story begins at dusk on a Friday evening and ends on the following Sunday morning. The month is October. In Ibsen's tradition of the well-made play, the opening scene presents a peaceful situation. Agnes, in her late fifties, cool, elegant and smooth, and her husband, Tobias, in his early sixties and recently retired, are engaged in what appears to be easy conversation while enjoying an after-dinner cordial. As one of the characters says later that weekend, "We submerge our truths, and have our sunsets on untroubled waters." The motif of a night-sea-journey is suggested as, little by little, this man and woman drop *personas* of kindness and politeness and let their true feelings emerge.

The benign surface first starts to ruffle at the mention of Agnes's dependent and alcoholic younger sister, Claire, who lives with the couple. Even before her appearance on the scene, it becomes apparent that this woman's presence in the household is a frequent, if not regular, source of friction and strife between husband and wife. Waves start forming with the news that Julia, their 36-year-old daughter, is about to come home again from what appears to be her fourth marriage debacle. The storm breaks shortly before the end of *Act One*, when Harry and Edna, best friends of the couple for nearly forty years, unexpectedly arrive at the front door and cryptically announce they are planning to move in. Imperceptibly, the naturalistic surface of the well-made play shifts. A surrealistic and somewhat dreamlike situation comes into relief.

By the beginning of *Act Two*, which takes place on Saturday evening, the atmosphere in the household of Agnes and Tobias is definitely tense. With the mysterious intrusion of their friends, Harry and Edna, on their hands, as well as the return to the nest of daughter, Julia, and the persistent irritating, if perspicacious, sideline commentary of sister Claire, the submerged truths are stirred up and become clearly visible on top of what turn out to be very troubled waters indeed. Central is the conflict which develops between Julia, who wants to have her room back in her parents' house, and Harry and Edna, who simultaneously and unconditionally claim their rights of friendship under her parents' roof. After a series of increasingly tumultuous confrontations among the six characters, and after the demons are all let out, the emptiness, resignation, and bitterness in the lives of these deeply unhappy people are painfully exposed. However, in my interpretation, the forces for psychic change and new consciousness are also mobilized for the future.

In his *œuvre*, Edward Albee is critical of the rigidity and sterility implicit in a conventional marriage, where an equal relationship between partners is doomed and real *eros* is impossible. Jung's description of such a marriage also fits the situation in *A Delicate Balance*. It is a marriage in which, as he puts it, "…a man's vital energy or Libido is focused almost entirely upon his business, so that as a husband he is glad to have no responsibilities. He gives the complete direction of his family life over to his wife…His real life (ie. his business) is where the fight is. The lazy part of his life is where his family is."[54] We may assume that, in his life as a businessman, Tobias was successful. He built his own house in the suburbs. There are unseen domestic servants in the background. Even a gardener is mentioned. In every material way, Tobias has been a good provider; all the comforts of modern living are clearly in evidence. For her part, Agnes seems to have managed the house impeccably and attended to all the details, "...food, and not just anything, and decent linen." A perfectionist, she has done her best to always look attractive and to assume whatever duties were demanded. She even describes herself as a stickler on points of manners, timing, tact, the graces—the one in charge of "maintenance." Was Agnes a monomaniacal Hestia?

Daughter Julia has grown up with all the advantages of a comfortable and well-organized material existence. From the author's description of the cast of characters, at the time of the action of the play, Julia is 36 years old. Although she is not yet physically present in *Act One*, there are frequent references to her in the opening sequences; by the time she appears at the beginning of *Act Two*, we know several things about her. First and foremost, she has trouble staying married. She is melancholy. Apparently, each of her marriages so far has lasted about three years, and each time after the break-up, with rhythmical regularity, she has returned home to her parents' house. As Jung says in his discussion of "The Significance of the Father in the Destiny of the Individual," "...the emotional relationship of a child to the parents, and

---

[54] *C.G. Jung Speaking: Interviews and Encounters*, eds. William McGuire and R.F.C. Hull (London: Pan Books, 1980), 39-40.

particularly to the father, is of decisive significance in regard to the content of any later neurosis. This relationship is indeed the infantile channel along which the libido flows back when it encounters any obstacles in later years, thus reactivating the long-forgotten psychic contents of childhood."[55]

Already in *Act One*, we see the parents' attitude has been that it is acceptable for Julia to return home, that home is where she belongs when she is not living with a husband. The mother, Agnes, is closest to the daughter, Julia; she is the one who speaks to her regularly on the telephone. It seems that, if she has not actually encouraged Julia to return, she has certainly not discouraged her: "I don't want her here, God knows. I mean she's welcome, of course...it is her home, we are her parents, the *two* of us, and we have our obligations to her . . ." Tobias, the father, appears to approve by default. He does not have contact with his daughter or any idea of what is going on in her life. Apparently, he hardly talks to her at all! His attitude is summed up when he says, "Hell, I don't know" to an inquiry by his sister-in-law. Claire's acerbic reply to this is, "It's only your daughter." Later, when Agnes comes back from the phone on this Friday evening to announce Julia is, in fact, about to leave her fourth husband and come home again, she makes the somewhat accusatory statement that Tobias has never talked to his daughter, nor to any of her husbands on previous occasions when there were difficulties, and he has not only neglected to make his child feel he cares about her, but that he has been virtually indifferent to her for years.

---

[55] C.G. Jung, "The Significance of the Father in the Destiny of the Individual," *Freud and Psychoanalysis*, CW 4, par. 693.

By the middle of *Act Two*, the implication is clear that daughter Julia keeps falling back into the childhood relationships she has never given up—particularly where her father is concerned. As Jung says, "It is ever so in life when we draw back before too great an obstacle, say the threat of some severe disappointment or the risk of some far-reaching decision. The energy stored up for the solution of the task flows back and the old riverbeds, the obstacle systems of the past, are filled up again."[56]

As the play progresses, we learn more about the circumstances surrounding Julia's early childhood. We learn about the death of her two-year-old brother, Teddy, and the effects of this sad event on the marriage of Agnes and Tobias; the shock, the pain, the grief and disappointment of this tragedy brought with them far-reaching changes in the lives of this couple. Gradually, Tobias turned away from intimacy with his wife. He would not let Agnes "take care of it." There would be no more children. Unable to deal with his emotions, Tobias's interests and energy flowed into his business, the office, his distinguished if "indistinguishable" friends in town, his clubs, and the "regulated great gray life," as his sister-in-law describes it. Tobias became physically and emotionally withdrawn from his wife, but also emotionally distant and inaccessible to his daughter.

We learn that, for Agnes, the estrangement from her husband took on a greater note of distress when, in the aftermath of the loss of the child, there was a suspicion her husband had been unfaithful to her. Near the end of *Act Two*,

---

[56] Ibid.

she says, "It was an unreal time. Ah, the things I doubted then: that I was loved—that *I* loved, for that matter!" Was Teddy the string which held them together? In any case, a vital emotional and sexual relationship between the partners came to an end—a relationship which Agnes can still remember with nostalgia.

At the time of this crisis in the family, Julia was about five or six years old. She recounts how she adored her father when she was a little girl. We also learn she felt tricked and betrayed when her baby brother, Teddy, was born, and suffered inordinate jealousy. After the boy's death, in addition to the reverberations of the collapse of the feeling and intimate life between her parents, it seems she also suffered terrible guilt, as if she had prayed her baby brother would go away and her prayers were answered. The death of Teddy, however, did not restore Julia to her father's undivided love. From that time on, a potent and penetrating masculine presence in the home disappeared, and the girl grew up in a prevailingly heavy and negative atmosphere.

As Jung points out, "The first signs of the later conflict between the parental constellation and the individual's longing for independence occur as a rule before the fifth year."[57] When Julia was around this age, the ground under her feet was shaken. Her mother, deeply troubled and overcome with feelings of insecurity and every imaginable doubt, was suffering from profound losses. In the meantime, her father had become emotionally and physically withdrawn. At around the time she would have been starting school, which

---

[57] Ibid., par. 701.

traditionally is the time when a child begins to take the first steps to move away from the narrower world of the mother and the home to enter the wider world of father and work, Tobias virtually absented himself from his family. He was not emotionally available to provide the necessary support to his daughter and function as her "bridge to the world."

In his discussion of the difficulties of a daughter in relation to her father, Jung says, "The glossing over of the family problem and the development of the negative parental character may take place deep within, unnoticed by anyone, in the form of inhibitions and conflicts which she does not understand." We learn that for Julia the repetition of the pattern of failed marriages had a precedent in a long series of failures at different schools. It is as if Jung is describing Julia when he continues, "As she grows up, she will come into conflict with the world of actualities, fitting in nowhere, and suffering from her own infantile and unadapted qualities."[58]

When we meet Julia in the first scene of *Act Two,* in Jung's words, she is returning to the source of an infantile disturbance involving her relationship to her parents and, as we shall see, in particular to her father. There is something almost grotesque about Julia as she demands to be taken in, bag and baggage, and to be catered to as if she were a misunderstood child. According to her chronological age, she is on the verge of the second-half-of-life! Underscoring her aimlessness and her lack of personal autonomy, Aunt Claire teasingly calls her a "perpetual brat."

---

[58] Ibid.

III

It is difficult to explore a relationship between a daughter and her father without also talking about her mother. Normally, it is the biological mother who is the first person in an infant's life. From the moment of conception and through at least the first year of life, the child is viscerally connected to the mother—warmed, nourished and protected by her. In an optimal primary relationship, the mother is the first person with whom the child feels safe and validated, and from whom she gains the sense of ground under her feet. As Erich Neumann describes it, "This embryonic and infantile relationship to the mother is the prototype of every *participation mystique.*"[59] There is certainly every indication that Agnes has done her best to be what she believes is a good mother. Until the weekend of the play, we know—in spite of her underlying disillusionment and discontent—Agnes has behaved maternally, and she has been available to Julia during each of the previous three times the young woman returned to her parents' house for succor after a divorce. There is also the implication that each time Julia failed out of a school, her mother took her back, and just as it is suggested she was involved in the choice of Julia's succession of husbands, Agnes was the one who selected the succession of new schools for

---

[59] See "The Psychological Stages of Feminine Development," trans. Hildegard Nagel and Jane Pratt (Spring, 1959), 64. This essay now also appears in *The Fear of the Feminine and Other Essays on Feminine Psychology* (Bollingen Series LXI-4), trans. Boris Matthews, Esther Doughty, Eugene Rolf, and Michael Cullingworth (Princeton, New Jersey: Princeton University Press, 1994).

her. Even earlier, during the period when Julia was a small child and coming home with bloody knees (Agnes says she wondered whether the girl was just clumsy or had been doing penance), the mother was the one who cleaned her up each time and dried her tears. There is no question about the emotional involvement of Agnes with her child. However, the real problem was never solved.

We know Agnes is very concerned about doing the right thing. For example, she says repeatedly that she is the only one in the family concerned with appropriate behavior. She does her best to live according to accepted values and tries to observe the approved customs and rules for a wife and mother. As Jung has pointed out, however, ". . . the things which have the most powerful effect upon children do not come from the conscious state of the parents but from their unconscious (and) the things we can manipulate more or less, namely consciousness and its contents, are seen to be ineffectual in comparison with these uncontrollable effects in the background, no matter how hard we may try."[60] The fact is, the psychic atmosphere in the home was disturbed. We may assume that, at least from the time Julia was starting school, if not before, she knew something was not right. Taking an unsentimental look at the real and debilitating problems in the marriage of Agnes and Tobias, why has Agnes been willing to deal again and again over the years with a growing and then a grown-up child without the support of her husband, as if Julia were still a child, and—in the process—somehow

---

[60] C.G. Jung, "Introduction to Wickes's 'Analyse der Kinderseele,'" *The Development of Personality*, CW 17, par. 84.

manage to keep her a child? What have been the needs of Agnes in this *symbiotic* mother-daughter relationship? In one of sister Claire's irritating sideline commentaries, she says in a mock drawl—perhaps assuming an outlandish accent to establish comic distance from a painful and awkward truth— that Agnes got Julia "hitched" each time just for the pleasure of getting her back.

It is impossible not to be struck by the emptiness of Agnes's life, a life which, by her own admission, she dedicated to the maintenance of "a shape—whether proud of the shape or not." We do not learn much about Agnes's background. Several clues, however, suggest she did not get along well with her own mother, that she was (and is) highly jealous of her younger sister, Claire, and that her attitude toward her father (and therefore patriarchal authority) was fundamentally obedient. In her marriage to Tobias, she accepted a tacit contract to attend to all the details of domestic life—all matters related to home and child. We can see that, whatever her real feelings were, by "putting up with" Agnes enabled a non-relationship with her husband, one which was polite but actually more like a transaction than an interaction, and lacking in a psychic connection.

Near the end of *Act Two*, Agnes refers to a ritual of mothering which she has gone through three times, each time her daughter came home again after a failed marriage—one which she anticipates going through again late that Saturday night. She says, "I'll lose myself once more." It feels like a ritual that, in its essence, is a continuation of the pattern of interrelation between mother and daughter, which goes back through a long series of bad reports and new schools and, even further back, of bloody knees. There is something sensuous in Agnes's description of "the four-hour talk . . . the soothing recapitulation." Her description of this ritual has an incestuous quality: ". . . a pat on the hand, a gentle massage . . . slowly, slowly combing the hair." The suggestion that Agnes has also received a sustaining personal and physical satisfaction from these extended sessions of mothering is unavoidable. Alas, her smoothing and straightening may also be interpreted as smothering. In other words, Agnes's mothering attitude over the years has been contributing to the blocking of change. All things considered, it does appear that, until the weekend of the play, Julia has remained "...fixated, held fast in an unripe form of her identity" in what Erich Neumann describes as the matriarchal phase of feminine development.[61]

At the psychological moment of Julia's arrival on Saturday, Agnes is having trouble keeping her peaceful, calm, managerial *persona* in place. In addition to her irritation with her sister, Claire, who is drinking again, she is highly edgy because of the mysterious invasion of "best friends" Harry and Edna, who in the meantime have barricaded themselves in Julia's old room. Preoccupied with the details of keeping her house in order, impatient and not open or receptive to her

---

[61] "Fear of the Feminine," trans. Irene Gad from Erich Neumann's essay, "Die Angst vor dem Weiblichen," which appears in *Die Angst: Studien aus dem C.G. Jung Institute, Zurich: Vortragszyklus des Winters 1958-1859* (Zurich: Rasher Verlag). It can be found ed. by Jeanne Walker in *Quadrant*, Vol. 19, No. 1 (Spring, 1986), 7-30. This essay also appears in *The Fear of the Feminine and Other Essays on Feminine Psychology*, Erich Neumann, trans. Boris Matthews, Esther Doughty, Eugene Rolf, and Michael Cullingworth (Bollingen Series LXI-4) (Princeton New Jersey: Princeton University Press, 1994).

daughter's surliness and neediness, during their first exchange on that weekend, some of the familiar dynamics between this mother and daughter are breaking down.

IV

In examining the conflicts aired during the action of *A Delicate Balance*, an impulse for change in the story of the play, which may not be overlooked, is that Tobias has stopped working. There is even a suggestion he retired somewhat early because of a medical problem. As Claire sarcastically points out, her brother-in-law is no longer engaged in "the regulated great gray life." We learn he putters in the garden, reads the newspaper and listens to classical music—no longer spending the days of his weeks in town with his work and his business friends. Although he still seems to be playing golf on the weekends, Tobias, in fact, is spending most of his time at home now—with his wife. Habits and attitudes which have prevailed for thirty to forty years are suddenly no longer relevant. At the beginning of *Act One*, Agnes already expresses her current standpoint in no uncertain terms when she says, "All the years we have put up with each other's wiles and crotchets have earned us each other's company." If Tobias has been "very sick . . . with the stomach business" recently, it appears that Agnes, too, is not prepared to stomach the pattern of a lifetime much longer. From the beginning of the play, the delicate balance of the *status quo* in this household is being challenged.

Early in *Act Two*, after a very unsatisfactory meeting between mother and daughter, when Tobias enters the room, Agnes, eager to attend to household organization, says to Julia, with more than a hint of irony in her voice, "Your mother has arrived. Talk to *him!*" She leaves father and daughter alone—to talk. Usually, it is the biological father who is the first man in a woman's life. Traveling away from home and coming back again, while the child remains safely with her mother, a father traditionally represents the world of work and school, of other people and other places. Ideally, commanding respect and obedience, he stands for authority and discipline. In relation to his occupation or profession, he represents goal, direction and focus—an active and dynamic principle of life. In an optimal father-daughter relationship, the male parent's love and interest in his child is crucial to her later development and to her adjustment and adaptation to the demands of her adult life. His loving participation in his daughter's upbringing fosters her self-confidence as well as her femininity. Gradually, with his encouragement and support, with the example of an emotionally involved father, a girl/young woman is weaned from the *participation mystique* with her mother and better able to move into the world of school, work, and eventually partnership on her own two feet. In this family, as we have seen so far, the father, Tobias, did not function as the bridge to reality for his daughter, Julia. He evaded the issue.

We learn that Tobias is quiet, predictable and stolid—courteous and eminently correct in his behavior. Not a demonstrative man, on the home front he is definitely nonassertive. We don't get a great deal of information about his background, although there is a suggestion that he was the son of a wealthy family and that he was cared for in his younger life at home by servants. Perhaps the real clue to his inner situation comes from a story he tells in *Act One* about an experience he had in the period before he met and married his wife.

When he was a bachelor, Tobias had a cat. At a certain moment he became aware she was turning away from him. He realized, too, that by the time he noticed it, it must have been going on for some time. Admitting he may have been neglectful, that his life had made demands, to correct the situation he tried to force the cat's attention—but only alienated her all the more. She hissed at him and bit hard. He struck the cat brutally on the head. In the end, out of frustration, he took her to a vet. He had the cat killed. When Tobias tells his story, we may wonder if here is an example of a man raised in a culture where boys aren't supposed to cry. We get the first real glimmering of his suffering as a man, as a husband and as a father, the first glimpse of his sense of emotional inadequacy and, by implication, of his wounded instinctual life. He says, "I hated her, well, 1 suppose because I was being accused of something, of failing. But I hadn't been cruel by design. I resented it. I resented having a . . . being judged. Being *betrayed*."

Tobias tells the story of the cat, which is so revealing about himself, after his sister-in-law, Claire, has prodded him about his indifference to his daughter, and after Agnes has come back from the telephone with the news Julia is returning home again from her fourth marriage. Tobias is the one who makes the connection between the difficulty he experiences talking to his daughter and the episode with the cat when he says, as if talking to himself, "If I saw some point to it, I might . . . if I saw some reason, chance. If I thought I might . . . break through to her, and say, 'Julia . . . ,' but then what would I say? Then nothing." Agnes, by this time, has very definitely said to him that she would laud it if he spoke to Julia's husband, as well: "If you've decided to assert yourself, finally, too late, I imagine... Julia might at the very least come to think her father cares, and that might be consolation—if not help."

Just before Agnes says to Tobias, "I wish you would (talk to Julia)!" there is another important hint about the complex *status quo* of this family in a stage direction, which reads *As if the opposite were expected from her*—the implication being that, more typically, Agnes would have said something like, "Don't bother," or "What's the point," or "*I'll* take care of it." However, on this evening, when she brings the news their daughter is expected home again, Agnes reiterates the sentiment she expressed earlier that evening in the opening scene of the play, when she says to Tobias, "All the years we have put up with each other's wiles and crotchets have earned us each other's company . . . I have reached an age, Tobias, when I wish we were always alone, you and I, without . . . hangers on . . . or anyone." There is no question the "hanger-on" is her sister, Claire, whose presence in the room at this moment Agnes is pretending to ignore. The "anyone" is Julia.

It is clearly inferred that Agnes's repeated readiness to accommodate her daughter's demands has also had to do with her own emotional needs. As long as Julia remains a daughter, Agnes is a mother. As long as there is a child in the house, Agnes and Tobias are a family. Until the evening on which the action of the play begins, Julia's lifelong neediness and her clockwork appearances have lent validity to the marriage of her parents. It seems, however, that since Tobias has retired and is spending most of his time at home, his wife is becoming less willing to accept his perennial attitude of non-involvement. With fateful irony, only moments after Agnes says to her husband, "I wish we were always alone," the family constellation is shaken to its foundations by the unexpected arrival at the front door of old friends, Harry and Edna.

V

Shortly before dinner on Saturday evening, after Agnes leaves Tobias and Julia alone, father and daughter have their first real encounter. Tobias too is edgy, puzzled by the mysterious presence of their friends in the house, and stressed by his wife's undisguised querulousness and pique. Is he feeling cornered by his sister-in-law's implied criticism of his indifference to his daughter's well-being? Perhaps he feels challenged by his wife's provocations. In any case, he takes a stand. When Julia riles him about his golf, he is suddenly quite blunt and—from her point of view—unexpectedly and disarmingly so. According to the stage directions, in this sequence *Tobias is surprisingly nasty:*

> "There are some times, when it all gathers
> up . . . too much. Some *times* when it's

134

going to be Agnes and Tobias, and not just Mother and Dad. Right? Some *times* when allowances aren't going to be made. What are you doing, biting your fingernails now? There are some *times* when it's all . . . too much. *I* don't know what the hell Harry and Edna are doing, sitting up in that bedroom! Claire is drinking, she and Agnes are at each other like a couple of . . . The goddamn government's at me over some deductions, and you! This isn't the first time, you know. This isn't the first time you've come back with one of your goddamned marriages on the rocks. Four. Count 'em. Four! You expect to come back here, nestle into being fifteen and misunderstood each time? You are thirty-six years old, for God's sake!... Thirty-six! Each time! Dragging your—I was going to say pride—your marriage with you like some Raggedy Ann doll, by the foot. You, you fill this house with your whining..."

Tobias is expressing his feelings. He is setting limits and, at the same time, showing Julia her boundaries. Assuming a position of authority *vis-à-vis* his daughter, his words are critical and disciplinary. He raises issues having to do with responsibility and choice. He lays down the law! In other words, Tobias is behaving like a good father.

At first, Julia is angry, stubborn and defiant. In fact, she becomes quite enraged. Sparks fly! Ultimately, though, after this outburst of emotion, father and daughter are able to engage in a lively exchange in which there is real contact.

Reflecting about her feelings for Tobias during her childhood and adolescence, Julia says, "As the years turned—poor old man—you sank to a cipher, and you've stayed there, I'm afraid—very nice but ineffectual, essential, but not-really-thought-of, gray . . . non-eminence." Then, as if she has done a double-take, gotten a closer look, and started scrutinizing with new eyes, she continues, "And now you've changed again, sea monster, ram! Nasty, violent, absolutely human man! Your transformations amaze me. How can I have changed so much? Or is it really you?"

As Jung describes it, ". . . emotion is the moment when steel meets flint and a spark is struck forth, for emotion is the chief source of consciousness. There is no change from darkness to light or from inertia to movement without emotion."[62] The confrontation between Tobias and Julia marks the crucial turning point in the relationship between this father and daughter. Ouranos is shoved aside, and the seeds are planted here for the future psychological development of Julia's personality. But also, for Tobias. If, in the first four years of her life, Julia grew up in a good-enough family, with the birth of her brother something happened. It is possible, in a culture which often places a higher value on sons than on daughters, Tobias loved his male child too much, or in a way which made the little girl feel excluded—less important. In any case, the birth of Teddy appears to have marked her expulsion from the paradise of childhood. The possibilities for a reasonable recovery from this shock were subsequently

---

[62] C.G. Jung, "Psychological Aspects of the Mother Archetype," *The Archetypes and the Collective Unconscious*, CW 9i, par. 179.

seriously impaired by Teddy's untimely death, and by the concomitant withdrawal of Tobias from the family. Dating from the period around the aftermath of her little brother's passing, when Julia was about six years old, for whatever complex reasons, the family became the lazy part of Tobias's life. From the time Julia would have been entering her first school year, if not before, although he was an excellent provider, Tobias was a weak father.

In the words of Erich Neumann: "Every single 'too much' or 'too little' which falls beyond the appropriate range will be experienced as negative by the child."[63] If we can imagine that in the psyche of a child there is a space—an emotional need for a mother and a father—when the father is absent, a vacuum forms. The space which he does not fill is invaded by the mother. "For instance," says Neumann, "an overpowering, binding mother who dominates the family situation will inhibit progress even with a father of normal strength. So too, a normally strong mother will become overpowering without any fault of her own in the presence of a particularly weak father figure, whose failure has a disturbing effect on the child's ego development."[64]

In his essay, "The Significance of the Father in the Life of the Individual," Jung emphasizes the powerful transpersonal aspects of the parents, that an archetypal Father and an archetypal Mother stand—as it were—behind the biological parents, exerting their force and their influence on the

---

[63] Erich Neumann, "Fear of the Feminine," trans. Irene Gad, ed. Jeanne Walker, *Quadrant*, Vol. 19, No. 1 (Spring, 1986), 7-30.
[64] Ibid., 14-15.

personality of the child. Here Jung is talking about the deleterious effects of an excessively dominating father figure.[65] In Julia's case, however, there has not been too much father, but not enough, and—as we can see—the emotional and physical absence of the personal father forms no less of an obstacle in the psychological development of the daughter than one who is too present and overbearing—the way Dr. Sloper was in the life of his daughter, Catherine, in *The Heiress*. It is the warming, nurturing, protecting and containing principles of the Mother that have predominated for Julia. With Tobias's detachment from his family, and specifically from the upbringing and education of his daughter, the Positive Father principles, for example, of spirit and intellect, reflection and will, have not constellated significantly. Julia's father did not encourage her to reach for the sky. Because of the increasing lack of participation by this father in his daughter's life, the positive aspects of mothering, so essential in the early years, take on a negative cast. The loving mother becomes excessively involved in her daughter's life, increasingly controlling and possessive—eventually even devouring. The girl's personal autonomy, her personal ambition and initiative, and her unique individual achievement are actually— however inadvertently—discouraged. Instead, passivity and dependency, and prevailing unconsciousness, are rewarded. Like a child of Ouranos, Julia's bridge to the world of personal autonomy has been blocked.

---

[65] C.G. Jung, *Freud and Psychoanalysis*, CW 4, pars. 728-729.

In his essay, "Psychological Stages of Feminine Development," Erich Neumann explains how masculine consciousness in the woman is born from the maternal unconscious.[66] In symbolic terms, as the child grows up, the gradual movement from the realm of the Mother to the world of the Father marks the development of consciousness and *ego* strength. When we meet Julia at thirty-six, she is still behaving like an adolescent. There is no indication she has finished some kind of education or that she has an occupation. Nor is there a hint she has an important friendship with a peer, or even a particular personal interest or hobby. Fundamentally passive and dependent, her attitude towards the future is provisional. On the verge of the second-half-of-life, Julia is still in a *participation mystique* with Agnes, entrenched in the matriarchal phase of her development. Without the presence of a father/ Father to support her evolution towards independence from her mother/Mother—without a real life of her own—Julia's inclination to *regress* remains strong.

VI

In *Act Two* of the play, following the antagonistic encounter between mother and daughter, and the emotional outburst between father and daughter, Julia has a less than

---

[66] Erich Neumann, "The Psychological Stages of Feminine Development," trans. Hildegard Nagel and Jane Pratt, *Spring*, 1959. This essay also appears in *The Fear of the Feminine and Other Essays on Feminine Psychology*, Erich Neumann, trans. Boris Matthews, Esther Doughty, Eugene Rolf, and Michael Cullingworth (Bolingen Series LXI-4) (Princeton New Jersey: Princeton University Press, 1994).

satisfactory meeting with her aunt Claire, who needles her niece about coming home again after another failed marriage. Claire says quite pointedly, "It's a great big world, baby. There are hotels, new cities…" Later in *Act Two*, after dinner, with her characteristic ironical wit, Claire cries out, "You're laying claim to the cave!" The "cave" is an apt symbol for a place of *regression* to an earlier stage of psychological and emotional development. As Neumann describes it, "…the feminine vessel character, originally of the cave, later of the house (the sense of being inside, of being sheltered, protected and warmed in the house) has always borne a relation to the original containment in the womb."[67] Thus, on the one hand, "cave" implies the generative, nourishing, protecting and warming character of the Earth and of the Mother. On the other hand, however, "cave" can also suggest a grave or a tomb, and the darkness of the underworld. The same Mother Earth which brings life forth, can take it back.

As Jung points out in *Symbols of Transformation*, "The more a person shrinks from adapting himself to reality, the greater becomes the fear which increasingly besets his path at every point. Thus, a vicious circle is formed: fear of life and people causes more shrinking back, and this in turn leads to infantilism."[68] Each time Julia returns to her parents' house from the world—from a failed school or a failed marriage—seeking reassurance and security, she is in effect retreating and hiding from the demands of adult life. The more her

---

[67] Erich Neumann, *The Great Mother*, trans. Ralph Mannheim (Princeton, NJ: Princeton University Press, 1963), 137, 149.
[68] C.G. Jung, "The Battle for the Deliverance from the Mother," CW 5, par. 456.

parents take the attitude expressed when Tobias also says in the long overdue emotional confrontation with his adult child, "YOU BELONG HERE!," the "cave," which in the beginning functions as the generative womb, gradually takes on the character of a grave—the grave of an individual soul.

As we've seen, Agnes, who married for better or worse, was disappointed by her husband. To the extent her marriage did not bring fulfillment to her as a wife, we can say she compensated for Tobias's lack of involvement with her and the family—and his lack of paternal feeling—by over-investing her maternal energy in her daughter. As a result, until the weekend of the play, the original nature of the psychic connection between this mother and daughter has prevailed far beyond the period of life when it is normal and advantageous for the mental health of either one of them. It is as if Agnes and Julia have remained stuck in a Demeter-Persephone pattern of relationship.

The fact that mother and daughter are the same gender complicates the psychological development of the feminine. In the simplest terms, in the first stage of life, a son identifies with his father or a father substitute, and also usually with a one-sided patriarchy, in order to be able to assume his responsibilities as a man in the society in which he lives. Traditionally, a daughter, to find her *Self*, identifies with the person who is the first woman in her life, her mother. Yet, at the same time, like a son, in order to develop consciousness, *ego* strength and personal autonomy, a daughter also needs to separate from the one-sidedness of the primary relationship. As Jung says, the young person requires much strength to wrench itself from its infantile past and venture into a strange world with all its unforeseen possibilities: "The whole of the libido is needed for the battle of life to follow the call of her individual destiny and to tear aside all sentimental attachments."[69] In other words, to get into life, a daughter needs at least a partial identification with her father. We have seen that Julia grew up feeling fundamentally unconnected to her personal father and therefore to the positive *masculine* principles which the archetypal Father, who stands behind him, represent. Without a real will of her own, Julia, at the age of 36, has remained a kind of extension of her mother. Edward Albee's play, *A Delicate Balance*, eloquently demonstrates the crucial importance of the inclusion of patriarchal as well as matriarchal identification in the upbringing and education of a daughter.

VII

The second act of *A Delicate Balance* is divided into two long scenes. In the first one, which takes place before dinner on the Saturday evening, Julia is much taken aback when she discovers ". . . the welcome-home committee (is) pretty skimpy . . ." Whatever the phone call on the previous evening might have promised, she meets a disagreeable and unempathetic mother who does not give her a chance to be heard. At the same time, she meets a father who unexpectedly penetrates

---

[69] Ibid., par. 463.

the awkwardness between them and talks to her sharply and critically, but also seriously and caringly. As she experiences the dependable and predictable attitudes of her parents breaking down around her, Julia's first reaction is, "Great Christ, what the hell did I come home to? And why? Both of you snotty, mean . . ." Her aunt Claire is not being sympathetic and supportive either, and on top of everything, suddenly and inexplicably, "godparents" Harry and Edna have taken over her old room. Their feeling about Julia's return to the very "nest" they are claiming as their own is hardly hospitable.

Looking at the play from the point of view of the character of the daughter, the climax or high point of the action on the weekend of Julia's return from her fourth marriage takes place later on that Saturday night near the end of *Act Two* when, crazily waving Tobias's pistol, Julia confronts Harry and Edna—and what they represent!—and demands that her father stand up for her and assure her of her rightful place in the family and in the home. "Get them out of here, Daddy!" she screams. "Get them out of here, Daddy!"

It is worth noting again that the sheer emotionality and potential for violence, which erupts near the end of *Act Two,* is already implicit in the first scene of *Act One,* when Agnes, however obliquely, expresses her dissatisfaction with the situation on the home front. Behind a facade of stylishness and self-control, she says to her husband, "What I find most astonishing is (the ingratitude of) Claire . . . and your reflex defense of everything that Claire (does)." In her long digression between the first and the second half of this statement, she muses about what it would be like to just "drift off" and go mad—to just get away from it all. Later, when her sister appears on the scene, Agnes leaves the living room to make her call to Julia in California. Still smarting from Agnes's recent verbal assault at dinner, Claire introduces a brutal fantasy. She says to her brother-in-law, ". . . why don't you . . . take a gun and blow all our heads off." Tobias, who picks it up immediately, says, "But it would have to be an act of passion," causing Claire to laugh out loud. There is more than a hint of underlying aggression and despair behind the bantering that goes on between these two and their sardonic exchange about a smoking gun and screams—and "brains lying around in the rugs."

On the next evening, at the beginning of the second scene of *Act Two*, after what Julia describes as "the ugliest dinner I have ever sat through," it is clear Agnes has put her gracious and decorous *persona* aside. She behaves instead in a rigid, opinionated and controlling manner. In this sequence Julia challenges her mother. She accuses her of behaving like "a combination . . . pope . . .and nanny" and mockingly calls her ". . . fulcrum and all around here, the double vision, the great balancing act." The exchange between mother and daughter becomes *surprisingly nasty*. Agnes says, "Well, why don't you run upstairs and claim your goddamn room back! Barricade yourself in there! Push a bureau in front of the door! Take Tobias's pistol while you're at it! Arm yourself!"

For Julia, with the "invasion" of Harry and Edna, it is as if a replay of the earlier trauma is set in motion. The long forgotten psychic contents of childhood have been reactivated. When the family friends take over her room, she relives the pain she suffered in the period surrounding first the birth and then the death of her brother, the time she felt "unwanted, tricked," and without reprieve from her father. Over thirty years later, though, the mother is unexpectedly not open and receptive to her child. Agnes does not offer Julia the unconditional warmth and protection her daughter has come to take for granted from her. However imperfect, the home that Julia knows and is accustomed to has suddenly turned into an unfamiliar and unfriendly place. Yet, in the flow of emotion that unexpectedly erupts between father and daughter earlier that Saturday evening, the ground for the re-establishment of their rapport is broken. Tobias shows interest and concern for his daughter again, and Julia, in spite of herself, is able to experience respect for him once more. This time it is Tobias who, however clumsily, assures her she belongs, when she does in fact "lay claim to the cave," and it is her father she calls to for help.

On Saturday evening after dinner, the atmosphere among the members of this family is volatile, especially after Harry and Edna, with their proprietary airs, rejoin them laden with luggage—which Tobias then obligingly carries up the stairs for them. As nobody else seems to be doing anything about what is happening, Julia is the one who takes a stand. Angry and resentful at the invasion of this couple, who are behaving as if they are taking over her parents' house, she does not quibble with ideals about the demands of friendship—much less her own personal, selfish and childish motives. She wants what is hers. She wants her room back! Unabashedly acting out her gut feelings, to everyone's embarrassment Julia makes a scene in front of the "guests." When it becomes clear her mother is not going to stand up for her, she rushes upstairs after Tobias calling, "Daddy? Daddy?" Matter-of-factly, Agnes observes, "Why, I do believe that's the first time [Julia's] called on her father in . . . since her childhood."

When Tobias rejoins the group in the living room, he expresses bewilderment and alarm at Julia's hysterical outburst, which he has just witnessed upstairs. Agnes, however, behaves as if she is impervious to what is going on. In her attitude, there is an echo of her words to Julia earlier that evening, when she says, "I do wish sometimes I had been born a man," and when she makes her sarcastic quip, "Well, there you are, Julia; your father may safely leave the room now, I think. Your mother has arrived. Talk to *him*!" Agnes, who has, after all, always taken care of family matters, and particularly the issues concerning Julia, is flatly refusing to do a thing. Tobias is shocked. "I haven't the time . . . I haven't the time for the four-hour talk," says Agnes, "the soothing recapitulation. You don't go through it, my love: the history . . . Oh my dear Tobias . . . my life has gone through more than hers. I see myself . . . growing old each time, see my own life passing. No, I haven't the time for it now. At midnight, maybe..."

The climax comes when, desperate and distraught, Julia comes down the stairs threatening Harry and Edna with a loaded gun, crying out again and again, "Get them out of here, Daddy!" At this point, in the midst of the confusion, Tobias takes charge. He remains calm and totally in control, for what he has to do is perfectly clear. With quiet firmness, he reclaims the weapon. There is a glimpse here of the side of Tobias that he has been cheating his family of for at least the past thirty years—the decisive man of authority and action. Julia's acting out may be described as histrionic and inappropriate, yet—however awkwardly, falteringly and belatedly—she is making a step in the direction of a psychological shift from the comforting and soothing of Mother to the firmness, direction and action of Father.

VIII

As Erich Neumann puts it, "The progress from the matriarchal phase to the patriarchal is trans-personal; it is the archetypal plan of the necessary maturation process embedded in the structure of each child." The role of the personal mother in supporting or preventing this process is of enormous consequence. It is the existence of a "supportive father figure," however, which is crucial in the child's "evolution towards independence and relative liberation from the mother."[70] When the previously dominating archetype constellates its negative side, the movement from one phase to the next is facilitated. As we have seen in the above discussion of *Act Two* of the play, Agnes becomes more like the Terrible Mother. At the same time, however, when she says to her daughter, "Arm yourself," she is encouraging Julia to claim her independence. "It is very helpful to understand," explains Neumann, "that one of the fundamental laws of the psyche is that the *Self* always

---

[70] Erich Neumann,"Fear of the Feminine," trans. Irene Gad, *Quadrant*, Vol. 19, No.1 (Spring, 1986), 7-30.

'dresses' or 'disguises' itself in the archetype of the progress-directed phase."[71] Julia is assuming a symbolically *masculine* disguise when, in order to overcome the Witch, with the help of Tobias's pistol, she asserts herself aggressively. The backup of the Father, which is represented by this attribute, as well as by the authoritative demonstration of genuine interest and concern by Tobias, help Julia now in her separation from the Mother and, potentially, with the help of some positive *animus*, also in her development into a more effective adult.

In *The Analysis of the Self*, where he addresses the consequences of severe maternal deprivation, Heinz Kohut also underscores the importance of the father in the destiny of the individual. Up to the weekend of the play, there is no suggestion of unreliability or unpredictability in the mothering of Agnes—on the contrary. However, as we have seen, eventually any "too much or too little" has a negative effect. Kohut shows how in the case of the maternally deprived child—in other words, where there is an extremely negative mother—if the father is able to respond empathetically to its needs, the child's adaptation to reality is made easier: "...if the father's personality is a firmly demarcated one and if he is able, for example, to let himself first be idealized by the child and then to allow the child gradually to detect his realistic limitations without withdrawing from the child, then the child may turn toward his wholesome influence, form a team with him against the mother, and escape relatively unscathed."[72] In

---

[71] Ibid., 10.

[72] Heinz Kohut, *The Analysis of the Self* (New York: International University Press, 1971), 66.

the course of *Act Two*, just like such a child, Julia starts to form a "team" with her father.

For a daughter, the first carrier of the counter-sexual element in her psyche is usually her biological father. Jung calls this inner man or "projection-making factor," which in its various aspects consists of the characteristics of a *masculine* being, the *animus*. As an archetype it embodies opposite poles. In an *inferior masculine* manifestation, for example, it may surface as an opinionated, argumentative and self-righteous manner. "No matter how friendly and obliging a woman's Eros may be," says Jung, "no logic on earth can shake her if she is ridden by the *animus*."[73] Could we describe this as a Kronos attitude? After all, when a woman is caught up in the *negative animus*, she knows she is right. An illustration of this can be observed in some of Agnes's manner, particularly in the scene after dinner on Saturday, which Julia mimics: "We will not discuss it"; "Claire, be still"; "No, Tobias, the table is not the proper place"; "Julia!" *Animus* can be described as the sum of conventional opinions. You can see *animus* in a woman when it manifests itself like the reactionary, conservative and intolerant posturing of the *inferior masculine*. These rigid and controlling ways make communication and a real relationship between people difficult—if not impossible. Jung describes the *animus* as "the deposit, as it were, of all woman's ancestral experiences of man . . ." But note. In his description of a superior or *positive* manifestation of the *animus*, he reminds us that the archetypal father/Father does

---

[73] C.G. Jung, "The Syzygy: Anima and Animus," *Aion*, CW 9ii, par. 29.

not only express itself in conventional opinions, but equally in ". . . what we call 'spirit,' philosophical or religious ideas in particular, or rather the attitude resulting from them . . . Just as the anima in a man becomes, through integration, the Eros of consciousness, so the animus becomes a Logos; and in the same way that the anima gives relationship and relatedness to a man's consciousness, the animus gives to a woman's consciousness a capacity for reflection, deliberation, and self-knowledge."[74]

Notice how Jung emphasizes that the meaning of "spirit" is not restricted to intellect: ". . . it is more, it is an attitude, the spirit by which one lives."[75] We talk, for example, about a lively spirit, a cheerful spirit, a courageous spirit, a curious spirit, a fighting spirit, or a spirit of adventure. Spirit may also be interpreted as the creative attitude which makes a woman want to experience the fullness of her life energy in her own independent and individual way. In the story of Julia and her emotionally absent Ouranos father, we have seen how Tobias's absence, his unavailability and indifference to his daughter, have not contributed to the development of her self-esteem or her sense of personal autonomy. She has suffered in her life from the feeling that her father did not really care about her. Without an internalized, forward-urging inner masculine aspect or *positive animus*, each time she came upon an obstacle in her path there was nowhere else she could go psychologically except back. In her case, that meant back

---

[74] Ibid., par. 33.
[75] C.G. Jung, "The Personification of the Opposites," *Mysterium Coniunctionis*, CW 14, par. 232.

home to her mother and to all the things Mother represents. But was she not also, at the same time, in search of her father/ Father?

On Friday evening, when Agnes returns from the telephone and announces, ". . . Julia is coming home," Tobias, meanwhile, having just been prompted by Claire, asks, "But wasn't Julia happy? You didn't tell me anything about..." As Jung reminds us, ". . . what has been spoiled by the father can only be made good by a father."[76] On Saturday, overcoming his reserve and fear of being "judged," Tobias does indeed "talk" to Julia. In the spirited exchange between them, sparks fly; father and daughter finally make emotional contact with one another. As if stepping back to take a closer look, and to take him in, Julia—somewhat incredulous—calls her father "...sea monster, ram! Nasty, violent, absolutely human man!"

A sea monster suggests Poseidon, whom Kerenyi describes as "a darker father beside his heavenly brother..."[77] A phallic-chthonic god, the sea monster is an image for instinctuality. Poseidon can also represent a great wave of emotion rising from the inner depths. On the other hand, the ram is a solar animal connected with the light of heaven, illumination and intellectual vision. This emblem of a sun god with its powerful horns represents fertility and creativity. He stands for assertiveness and pugnacity. Perhaps most important of all, the ram symbolizes the overthrowing of the old order and the quest for an independent and individual

---

[76] Ibid.

[77] Carl Kerenyi, *The Gods of the Greeks* (Middlesex, England: Penguin Books Ltd., 1958), 160-161.

spiritual identity—the adventurous search for the true father within.[78] The images of these two divine figures, each with its respective transformative qualities, bring together opposite poles of the masculine principle. "Even a so-called 'ideal spirit' is not always the best," Jung tells us, "if it does not understand how to deal adequately with nature, that is, with the animal man."[79] Numinous and transpersonal, the sea monster and the ram together symbolize not only spiritual strength, but also powerful instincts and emotions.

IX

It appears that, during the confrontation with her father, Julia experiences an awakening. Vital and dynamic, supportive *animus* aspects begin to constellate in her *psyche*; her *ego* strength and consciousness are deepened and broadened. On the weekend of the play, however awkwardly, Julia stands up to the interlopers, Harry and Edna—and what they represent. She calls on her father for recognition and acceptance and claims her place in the family. The scenes she makes and the stir she causes imply not only an achievement for her *ego*, but they also contribute to an emotional breakthrough for all the members of the household assembled on this Saturday evening. As we have seen, from about the time Julia was six years old, she did not really know her father. She did not

---

[78]Liz Green, *The Astrology of Fate* (York Beach, Maine: Samuel Weiser, Inc., 1986), 176-182.

[79] C.G. Jung, "The Personification of the Opposites," CW 14, par. 232.

experience him as a strong positive *masculine* influence, much less as a "sea-monster" or a sun god. A Puella, her viability in the real world remained weak. She was like an eternal girl. If each of her marriages lasted three years, she must have been twenty-one or younger the first time she moved from her parents' house. There is no evidence she ever lived on her own or supported herself before she left home, and there is even an implication that Agnes played a role in arranging at least one of her daughter's marriages.

We know very little about Julia's husbands—or why her first three marriages ended in divorce. Aunt Claire gives some clues in a *mocking sing-song*: "Philip loved to gamble, Charlie loved the boys, Tom went after women, Douglas..." Perhaps an indication of the immaturity of Julia's *animus—animus* now as ego-consciousness and as projection-making factor—can be found by examining the personalities of the men she married. Here I am indebted to Barbara Greenfield's witty interpretation and discussion of the different forms the archetypal masculine takes which correspond to various stages of feminine *ego* development.[80]

Looking at Julia's husbands—Philip, Charlie, and Tom—as Trickster, Puer, and Don Juan respectively, they appear to represent less psychologically developed, early stages of the *masculine*. Philip, the gambler, suggests the Trickster, who has symbolic significance as law-breaker and liberator. Perhaps it is also significant that it is his name which Agnes cannot

---

[80] Barbara Greenfield, "The Archetypal Masculine: Its Manifestation in Myth, and Its Significance for Women," *The Father: Contemporary Jungian Perspectives*, ed. Andrew Samuels (London: Free Association Books, 1985), 187-210.

remember. Mercurial and adventurous, the Trickster is also unreliable and lacking in self-control. Philip was able to seduce this daughter away from her mother, but he could hardly have lived up to being an optimal partner in a conventional marriage. Charlie, the second husband, who "loved the boys," suggests a Puer—in this case, an androgynous young man attractive to both sexes. It is interesting to note he was the match that Agnes arranged for Julia. Perhaps his boyishness appealed to her maternal feelings. Julia does say, much to Tobias's chagrin, that had her brother, Teddy, lived, he would have turned out to be like Charlie. Typically, a Puer has great charm and he is not threatening. It is possible to imagine, however, that too much mother-in-law—in addition to Julia's fundamental insecurity and dependency—drove him away. Tom, the third husband, who "went after women," suggests the Don Juan, a fellow with plenty of sexual energy and initiative. Paradoxically, his fascination with women implies he too is mother-bound. Self-centered and aloof, a Don Juan does not make a commitment or engage in a serious relationship with a peer. Looked at in this light, we can imagine Julia's first three husbands were immature young men lacking in real ego-strength and in a responsible sense of purpose and direction. In many ways, they were not unlike Julia herself.

In Erich Neumann's view, where masculine consciousness has not developed sufficiently out of the maternal unconscious, and "where the matriarchal or the maternal dominate, a complete meeting between man and woman is impossible."[81]

---

[81] Erich Neumann, "The Psychological Stages of Feminine Development," trans. Hildegard Nagel and Jane Pratt (*Spring*, 1959), 68.

After Julia has experienced positive adult contact with her father, and after she has been able to feel admiration for him again—as well as appreciation for him as an ordinary human being—it is possible that in the future her attitude toward a potential partner will change. Perhaps with the boost she gets in her self-esteem when she realizes her father does care about her, her ability to have a relationship with an outer man, or to the *masculine* principle within herself, has improved. Shortly after the scene of confrontation with her father, Julia says to her Aunt Claire, "I have *left* Doug. We are not *divorced.*" In Neumann's view, a woman's "...gaining the freedom to become conscious is tied up with the person of the hero."[82] At the end of the play, it remains open whether Julia's fourth husband will turn out to be a hero. In other words, it is unclear whether he will become a mature and active young man of will and intelligence, spirit and creativity, with whom she is going to be able to have a workable adult relationship—a love relationship that supports psychic healing for both partners.

X

Perhaps one of the most ironic lines in *A Delicate Balance* is spoken by the family friend, Edna, when, in the second half of *Act Two,* she scolds and provokes Julia. She says, "You've not helped wedlock's image any, with your shenanigans." The question of marriage and the problems of

---

[82] Ibid., 77.

marriage overshadow this play. Harry and Edna are described as *very much like Agnes and Tobias.* It helps to understand these two characters and their unexpected appearance on this autumn weekend, if we look at them not only concretely as long-time friends, but also as embodiments of *shadow* aspects of Agnes and Tobias. Harry and Edna function as personifications of aspects of the personalities and lives of their hosts, particularly the negative ones which have not been consciously confronted, but rather covered over by a facade of gracious living and *personas* of polite civility. As Jung assures us, "Happily, nature sees to it that the unconscious contents will erupt into consciousness sooner or later and create the necessary confusion."[83] Apparently, it was while they were sitting at home after dinner on Friday evening that Harry and Edna suddenly found themselves feeling scared. "WE WERE FRIGHTENED," cries Edna, "AND THERE WAS NOTHING." In the grip of their loneliness and fundamental discontent, it was as if the emptiness of their lives as a couple opened out before them like a great gaping void. There was nothing between them. There was nothing before them. Unexpectedly, and at a very inconvenient moment, these are the very people who appear at the front door of Agnes and Tobias. As autonomous *shadow* aspects are so often apt to do, they demand to be acknowledged and taken in. The irony is compounded when Tobias carries the suitcases of Harry and Edna upstairs to Julia's former room, just when this daughter is seeking her father's recognition and acceptance in her

---

[83] C.G. Jung, "The Conjunction," *Mysterium Coniunctionis*, CW 4, par. 672.

childhood home. If, on the one hand, the emotional sterility in the lives of Harry and Edna is perhaps represented by their childlessness, on the other hand, the lives of Agnes and Tobias have not become less barren because they raised a daughter. Tobias carries the baggage of a couple who represent the failure of a marriage relationship to the room of his daughter who has a problem staying married.

Neither Harry and Edna nor Agnes and Tobias have provided an exemplary model for a fruitful joining. Each man and each woman—well into the third half of life—has remained locked into his and her respective gender and social roles. In these lives without passion and lacking in *eros*, there has been no confrontation, no meeting between peers—no individuation. Edna sums it up later, in *Act Three*, when she says,

> "It's sad to know you've gone through it all, or most of it, without . . . that the one body you've wrapped your arms around . . . the only skin you've ever known . . . is your own—and it's dry . . . and not warm."

Agnes answers her:

> "Time. Time happens, I suppose. To people. Everything becomes too late, finally. You know it's going on . . . up on the hill; you can see the dust, and hear the cries, and the steel . . . but you wait; and time happens. When you *do* go, sword, shield . . . finally . . . there's nothing there . . . save rust; bones; and the wind."

It is late for Agnes and Tobias, and for their friends. It is not too late for Julia. On any level, it is impossible for her to tolerate the invasion of Harry and Edna. As the youngest person in the household, who is still the carrier of hope and future possibilities, for Julia to accept that Harry and Edna move into her house, sleep in her room, and "take over" would symbolize not only her acceptance of defeat and total resignation, but that of her parents as well.

XI

Act Three of *A Delicate Balance* begins early Sunday morning. After the upheaval and the chaos of the night before, the atmosphere in the household is subdued. The unwelcome intrusion of Harry and Edna has forced Agnes and Tobias to be more relaxed with one another: Since "best friends" slept in Julia's room, Julia had to sleep in her father's room, and Tobias had to move in with Agnes. At seven-thirty a.m., before anyone else is up, among the ruins of empty glasses and unemptied ashtrays, husband and wife sit in the living room and have a difficult and painful conversation. Agnes confronts Tobias with his emotional inadequacy: When he did not have things the way he wanted them, he did not deal with them. There is an echo of the story of Tobias and the cat. "The theory being pat," says Agnes, "that half a loaf is worse than none." However tacitly, Tobias does acknowledge that, over the years, he has let his wife down and neglected his child. At the end of the play, after Harry and Edna have left, without feeling judged or betrayed, Tobias is able to say, "I'm sorry. I apologize."

For her part, Agnes has understood that she did not take up "sword and shield" when she had the opportunity to assert herself. By accepting a life as an adjunct and by obediently doing what was expected of her according to rules and conventions outside of her *Self* and, along the way, not expressing her true feelings to her husband, Agnes not only let herself down, but her family as well. She enabled the *status quo* to prevail. On this occasion, however, where Harry and Edna are concerned, although she leaves the decision to Tobias, she states a preference. Already in *Act One* it is implied she would like to be less Mother and more Wife. She certainly does not want the "disease," which is what Harry and Edna represent to her, in her home. She does not want the "plague" of emptiness and despair to take over the life she and Tobias still have ahead of them in their "declining years."

For Tobias, the emotional climax comes later that Sunday morning when he stands face-to-face with Harry. During this encounter with his *shadow*/friend of four decades, with horror and exuberance he releases emotions, which, as the stage directions explain, he has *kept under control for too long*. When Tobias addresses Harry and the issue of the "invasion," he finally confronts his own limitations and his private failures. It is a heart-rending struggle this man goes through as he tries to come to terms with his theories and ideas about the way things should be, and the eruption of the disturbing experience of how he really feels: "STAY HERE!" he cries. "YOU'VE GOT THE RIGHT! YOU BRING YOUR PLAGUE! YOU STAY WITH US! I DON'T WANT YOU HERE! I DON'T LOVE YOU! BUT BY GOD...YOU STAY."

Referring to this tormented scene, Edward Albee has said, "Tobias can no longer fill his life with the problem of making an important choice. He cries, 'Dilemma, come back!' But it is too late."[84] In the meantime, however, Harry and Edna—and what they represent—have been admitted; they have been acknowledged and let in. There is no more pretense. Near the end of the play, as the invaders quietly depart of their own free will, Agnes and Tobias can look forward to an opportunity to renew and revitalize their personal connection on a deeper level of consciousness. And intimacy?

By the time everything's out in the open and the skeletons in the closet have been aired, and after Tobias and Harry have had their confrontation, Julia and Tobias have both suffered feelings of humiliation. As James Hillman puts it, "To be weak and helpless in one's feelings, to stand loyal with one's negative feelings, to be delivered over to one's childishness—and this in front of another person—is indeed humiliating."[85] Perhaps, ultimately, it is the facing and the admission of emotional inadequacy that fosters the humbling realization one is just an ordinary human being after all, and that that's OK.

The renewal of feeling and *eros* in the family can indeed be observed in the second scene of *Act Three* in Julia's animation as she presides over the coffee cups. Here, the teaming up of father and daughter becomes apparent. It is "Julie" this and "Pops" that. First, though, before she prepares the coffee, Julia makes a point of apologizing. "I'm sorry about last night,

---

[84] *Life* (28 October 1966), 120.
[85] See Marie Louise von Franz and James Hillman, "The Feeling Function," *Lecture on Jung's Typology* (Zurich: Spring Publications, 1971), 120.

Daddy," she says. "I mean I'm sorry for having embarrassed you." Then, rather disconcertingly for Tobias, she adds, "Aren't you sorry for embarrassing me, too?" By the end of the play there is something between Julia and her father.

After Harry and Edna leave and the family is alone together again, Tobias says, "I tried. I was honest. Didn't I? Wasn't I?" Julia answers, "You were very honest, Father. And you tried." She respectfully calls him "Father." She lets him know she accepts him with his limitations and does not judge him. Tobias, for whom showing his feelings and expressing emotion are so difficult, does not withdraw.

The renewal of *eros* in the family can also be seen in the less assertive, more gentle manner of Agnes and, as the play draws to a close, in the quieter and more reflective manner and tone of Claire. She even says she may be taking a vacation soon! The story behind Claire's permanent presence in the household is vague, the implication being that Agnes obediently—and literal-mindedly—kept a deathbed promise to their father to look after her younger sibling, and that Tobias went along with it. We can see these two imposing women as *shadow* sisters, representing opposite aspects of one personality. Rivals to the core, Agnes boasts about her loyalty to the system, while Claire has a reputation for promiscuity. Agnes, the epitome of management and control, is a perfectionist and a conformist—the "drill-sergeant" as Julia calls her. Claire—the one who sees everything (and does nothing!)—is extravagant and unconventional. Her serious problem with alcohol emphasizes a lifelong aimlessness and dependency. As unintegrated *shadow* aspects of one another,

Agnes and Claire forever get in each other's way, causing not only embarrassment but also prevailing discord in the family. Tobias, unhappily caught between the homemaker and the trouble-maker, has suffered from the split in the *feminine* in his own psyche. When the play ends, though, the atmosphere between the two women, which in the beginning was so poisonous, has become more relaxed. There is less animosity; humor and compassion are in the air. Perhaps the sisters have even become a little more understanding and accepting of each other—closer?

When Agnes and Tobias and Claire and Julia are all together at the end of the play, the question remains whether Julia's "laying claim to the cave" should be perceived as the death of a soul or—after all the emotional confrontations—whether her homecoming this time represents an opportunity for new consciousness, renewal and rebirth. Does her reinstatement in the bosom of the family stand for *regression* or, in Jung's words, it is "a purposive introversion of libido directed toward a goal"?[86] As we have seen, throughout the course of the weekend in the play, changes appear to have occurred in the relationships among all the members of this family, and—particularly where Julia and her father are concerned—certain things are no longer the way they were.

At the beginning of *Act Three*, Agnes herself underscores Julia's psychological shift from the realm of Mother to the world of Father, when she tells Tobias she did not have the usual long late-in-the-night talk with her daughter after all: "No, she wouldn't let me stay. 'Look to your own house,' is

---

[86] C.G. Jung, *Symbols of Transformation*, CW 5, par. 519.

what she said." Julia, knowing now that her father does care about her, can reject Agnes's mothering, and her smoothing and smothering, but also the role of the passive, dependent child. In the lively second sequence of *Act Three*, Julia not only assumes the womanly duties of early morning hostess, but also an attitude of authority *vis-a-vis* her mother, and even an attitude of competition *vis-a-vis* her aunt Claire. Julia's alliance is now clearly with Tobias. Could a danger be that, after having found her father again, the young woman might remain stuck in this new rapport?

From the beginning, Agnes expresses her desire for new life in her marriage, even though, when she goes to the phone to call her daughter in *Act One*, her motivation is ambivalent. Her concern for Julia appears to be connected to her own need for comfort. Ironically, although she accuses Tobias of never having taken a stand with Julia and his daughter's problem with marriage, Agnes is the one who has always offered the avenue of least resistance. She says at one point, "Julia has (divorces) for all of us." However, until the weekend of the play—when Agnes demonstratively leaves Tobias alone with Julia to talk—this mother has tried to keep her daughter for herself. In the end, it is doubtful she will encourage Julia to remain as a permanent live-in member of the family. Agnes feels the need for separation strongly. Remember, she says to Tobias, "I have reached an age . . . when I wish we were always alone, you and I, without . . . hangers-on . . . or anyone."

Before Harry and Edna leave on Sunday morning, when Edna asks her if she will be "seeing" Doug, Julia answers in an evasive and non-committal way—keeping counsel with herself. We learn that before her mother called her, Julia was not planning to come home that weekend. She says to Claire, "I have *left* Doug. We are not *divorced*..." In the scene after dinner on Saturday evening, when Julia is fed up with her mother's unrelatedness, she appears to be thinking about Doug. Having been married three times, and each time to a man who can be described as embodying a different early stage of *masculine* development, Julia's three marriages can also be seen to represent movement and gradual change. Doug is the fourth husband. Four symbolizes the qualities of the one, end and beginning. Four suggests an orientation towards wholeness—the unifying of diverging opposites. Thus, four also points to the activation of the *Self*.

There is little information about Douglas except that he is "against everything." If this man is merely negative, it would appear he did not represent progress for Julia. However, perhaps Doug is a man of ideas and originality, purpose and direction. In that case, it is possible to surmise he may still turn out to be a challenging and dynamic partner for Julia, the hero who can help her break out of the family complex, foster her own personal values, accept love, and start a viable life and perhaps a family of her own. The most optimistic reading would be that, in the future, Julia and Doug will be able to experience a life-changing encounter, a meeting of equals—individual to individual.

Jung has commented, "Any essential change, or even a slight improvement, has always been a miracle."[87] Just before

---

[87] C.G. Jung, "The Soul and Death," *The Structure and Dynamics of the Psyche*, CW 8, par. 815.

the curtain falls on this play, there is a delicate balance on another level of experience. Agnes talks about the wonder of the daylight and the sun after a night of darkness and confusion, when all the demons emerged from the deep. The dawning of Sunday, the rising sun at the end of the play, suggests new consciousness for all and the opportunity for unexplored possibilities in the future.

When Julia says, "You were very honest, Father. You tried," there is peace between this daughter and her father. Tobias has been available to Julia, and Julia has been receptive to Tobias in all his ordinary humanness. Perhaps there will be a pause now—a *reculer pour mieux sauter*—for the transpersonal Father to work in her as well, the spirit of the sun-god and of the sea-monster, the spirit of a supportive, heroic *animus*—and more. At the end of *A Delicate Balance*, there is a stillness between Julia and Tobias. Talking about the responsibilities of a father to a daughter and the kind of spirit a daughter needs, Jung says, "They are the truths which speak to the soul, which are not too loud and do not insist too much but reach the individual in silence—the individual who constitutes the meaning of the world. It is the knowledge that the daughter needs, in order to pass it on to her son,"[88] And to her daughter! Perhaps experiencing spirit, and the creative stillness—becoming more understanding, reflective and thoughtful—Julia will be better able to pick up her own life again, adapt to the demands of her personal and private reality, and assume the responsibilities of a mature human being.

---

[88] C.G. Jung, "The Personification of the Opposites," *Mysterium Coniunctionis*, CW 14, par. 233.

"Emotion is the moment when steel meets flint and a spark is struck forth, for emotion is the chief source of consciousness. There is no change from darkness to light or from inertia to movement without emotion."

- C.G. Jung

Concluding Remarks

There is a big difference between interpreting literary characters from the point of view of analytical psychology, and actually working face-to-face with a complex human being in the analytical vessel. However, talking about the negative effects a father's reactions and attitudes can have on his daughter—where an Ouranos or a Kronos, or a Negative Zeus Father are constellated in a woman's *psyche*—the archetypal aspect of plays like *The Heiress* and *A Delicate Balance* come to mind, and this is where it can be helpful to introduce the story of Catherine or Julia into the conversation.

When either the patriarchal or the matriarchal dominate in a daughter's *psyche*, positive *masculine* consciousness does not mature sufficiently out of the maternal unconscious for there to be an optimal meeting between *feminine* and *masculine* principles. In other words, it becomes difficult for a well-integrated, whole human being to develop—outwardly or intra-psychically. In a home atmosphere where *eros* is lacking, where there is inadequate or incompetent fathering combined with absent or passive, silent mothering, the balance is off. There will always be the danger that a daughter's talents and possibilities for the future will remain dormant or fade away in self-doubt. As she gets older, her unlived life can cause her a variety of psychological problems.

When a father withdraws from the family and does not give loving attention to his daughter, or when he presents himself as an overbearing patriarch, he is neglecting to support his child in the natural process of separation from the mother/Mother; he is not helping her to gain personal autonomy and an individuated life of her own. In our discussions of *The Heiress* and *A Delicate Balance*, we have seen how too much or too little parenting can have this damaging effect on *ego* development, as well as on an over-all sense of well-being. In her adult life, such a daughter will likely find herself in a place that has not been directed from within by her unique potential for wholeness, but rather dictated by the limiting one-sided, collective expectations of her particular family and the patriarchal culture around her.

In *Educated*, a recent, disturbing memoir about growing up in the Idaho mountains in an isolated, fundamentalist family, Tara Westover describes a father who embodies in the extreme the destructive forces of a compound archetypal Negative Father, and a mother who is a totally silenced Metis—almost to the point where they feel like caricatures. But there is nothing funny about this book, which gives a shattering glimpse into the other America—perhaps not as insignificant or as peripheral as many of us would like to think it is. *Educated* is raw testimony to a young woman's determination and perseverance to defeat incredible psychological, emotional and cultural obstacles.

The youngest of seven children, Westover did not have a birth certificate. She was never seen by a medical professional. Home schooled, as a child she was forced to work in her father's scrap-metal business, where she was casually exposed to life-threatening dangers and injuries. When she was a teenager, a sadistic older brother abused her, physically and psychologically, while the parents virtually looked on. That she was able to overcome her survivalist childhood—including the archetypal hazards of loyalty and obedience to family—as intact as she was, is a wonder to me. However, intellectually gifted, and with the serious encouragement of a supportive and caring older brother who had left the family (an older brother who, we could say, functioned as a surrogate positive father), she was able to teach herself what she needed to know to pass the SAT exams, break out of the restrictions imposed by her family, and go to college.

When years later she is at Harvard, working on a PhD in History, her parents come all the way from Idaho to visit her in her tiny dorm room at Cambridge. Their single-minded purpose is to save her soul. Westover describes how her father put a vial of consecrated oil into her hand and, practically breathing in her face, said, "I will offer, one final time, to give you a blessing." Westover writes:

> "Everything I had worked for, all my years of study, had been to purchase for myself this one privilege: to see and experience more truths than those given to me by my father, and to use those truths to evaluate my own mind. I had come to believe that the ability to evaluate many ideas, many histories,

many points of view, was at the heart of
what it means to self-create. If I yielded
now, I would lose more than an argument.
I would lose the custody of my own mind.
This was the price I was being asked to pay,
I understood that now. What my father
wanted to caste from me wasn't a demon:
it was me."[89]

The daughter replied: "I love you. But I can't. I'm sorry
Dad." This is the moment where Westover in fact separates
from the narrow, perilous world of her parents, and estranges
herself from most of her family of origin. Her mother refuses
to ever see her daughter again—until she shows respect for
her father. At the end of the book, highlighting the intensity
of her continuing inner struggle, Westover tells us she knows
that a part of her will always believe her father's words should
be her own. In this compelling, contemporary American
memoir, the author demonstrates the alarmingly powerful
and prevailing negative influence the archetypal dynamic
behind a father's embodiment and expression of authority
can have on the psyche of a daughter. Westover realizes that
to be herself, who she—as a unique individual—is capable of
becoming, she must leave her survivalist upbringing and her
father behind, find her authority within, and speak with her
own voice.

Near the end of *The Heiress*, Catherine says to her father,
"You cheated me." We saw how Dr. Sloper—a man of laws
and rules—did not want his daughter to make her own

---

[89] Tara Westover, *Educated* (New York: Random House, 2018), 304.

choices or mistakes. But a whole person does not mean a perfect person, and—as some would say—love is suffering. For sure, *Individuation* is suffering. Granted, this father is in a difficult position, for a crucial life-changing decision affecting three people is about to be made. However, having forgotten what it was like to be young and in love, in his over-protectiveness, the doctor did not try to support his child's happiness by giving her suitor a chance. For example, another father might have told the young man, "Yes, you can marry my daughter, providing you come back in a year with a job, and evidence you can support a wife and family by your own means." If Morris demonstrated that he was unwilling to accept this "bitter cup," the question of whether he was in a category from which to choose a son-in-law would have been cleared up in no time.

It is thought-provoking when, near the end of *Act One* of the play, Aunt Elizabeth, the mother of many children, suggests that we never know about these things—how Morris, for example, might have reacted to being married to Catherine. As a young woman raised in a Victorian climate, Catherine seems pretty well-informed about animal body parts, as well as lingerie and lavender—and baby clothes. She knows what she wants. Perhaps, with her love, she could have helped Morris to become a more grounded, self-confident man? But then it would have been a different play!

Whether he cuts off his daughter's head or her inheri-tance, or simply cuts off the possibility of a personal, supportive relationship with her, a negative father is desperate to be in control. We know about this from the archetypal, mythological family life of the pre-Olympian gods, and the various menages of Zeus—all described by Hesiod in *Theogony*. We have also seen how this need to control betrays psychological and social insecurity—which certainly comes across in the archetypal stories of Dr. Sloper and Tobias.

We are never told anything about the doctor's early years, except we know Sloper married a woman with money and that—with his strong ethical sense of responsibility— he built his fortune on top of her dowry. About Tobias, we hear he was raised by servants, which doesn't sound as if he was brought up in a conventional home. When we first meet these two fathers, they are emotionally fragile men—frozen in their *eros* by the trauma and suffering from the loss of a loved one. Are they afraid to give love again—to feel passionately— because trusting makes them vulnerable? In a culture where it is taboo for a man to show weakness, we watch how Dr. Sloper postures and defends, and how Tobias withholds and avoids. Are these two men wounded in their feeling-life because of their personal experience, or because of collective pressures—or both?

It is possible to love too much, to grieve too much and to get stuck in the past. When we meet Sloper and Tobias, neither of them has differentiated between going forward in life and getting on with their lives emotionally. As Jung has said, ". . . emotion is the chief source of consciousness. There is no change...without emotion."[90] In *The Heiress*, when Dr.

---

[90] C.G. Jung, "Psychological Aspects of the Mother Archetype," *The Archetypes and the Collective Unconscious,* CW 9i, par. 179.

Sloper loses control of Catherine, it seems he has nothing to live for anymore. At the end of *A Delicate Balance*, however, there is the possibility of redemption and healing. Ultimately, Tobias does risk showing his true feelings, and—letting himself surrender to his emotional confusion—he admits his failures, trusting that Julia and the family will accept him without judgement.

From Hesiod's *Theogony*, we also learn that when a daughter is born, she brings with her from antiquity not clouds of glory, but an archetypal inheritance of misogyny. To a greater or lesser degree—depending on her personal family and the collective values of her particular patriarchal culture—historically, she is born to be kept in a designated lower and more limited and limiting place. Again, depending on who her parents are, and where and when she is living, if she rejects subordination she will verily be kept or put in her place. Punished?

Misogyny supports sexism. Currently, in the greater collective, with all the apparent progress, and many outer changes in attitudes and reactions, we still do not have to look too closely to see man's lack of respect for woman, to the extent there are girls and women today who, for a variety of reasons—feeling this too—no longer want to be identified as female. Whether a patriarchal system is denying girls and women a decent education, or access to reliable health care, daughters are not always encouraged to strive for personal autonomy. Many women still are not allowed to have authority over their own minds and bodies, make their own mistakes and learn from life for themselves. In the greater collective, daughters are not being prepared to do this—not by their school or church, and—most importantly—not by their parents. Particularly not by their fathers.

Often, how a father treats his daughter will have an effect on the way a woman accepts or does not accept being treated badly by her husband—or by men in general. We are aware of the enormity and pervasiveness of the problem of sexual harassment. The statistics on domestic violence and rape in the United States are shocking. At the time of this writing, according to Google, one in four women in the US will be victims of domestic violence, and it is estimated that annually one in six women will be raped. Certainly, the appearance on television of such a diversity of bright, articulate professional women presenting, commenting and reporting on what is going on in the world is encouraging, but—in the big picture—these images are deceptive. Negative Father law may appear to be threatened, but it continues to rule.

In social media, prioritizing financial profit over supporting the greater good, a major corporation like Facebook, in their postings, gets away with knowingly harming young women. Marc Zuckerberg himself continues to downplay Instagram's effect on mental health, even though his own company's research shows that "Instagram makes millions of teen girls 'feel worse' about their body image."[91]

In contemporary pop culture, there is the grotesque example of Negative Father rule in the case of multi-

---

[91] See THE WEEK, October 1, 2021, 34.

millionaire entertainer, Britney Spears. At the age of 39, and after thirteen years and notorious legal battles, she has finally been released by the courts from the conservancy of her controlling father, Jamie Spears.[92] Will we ever know the truth behind that complex story?

In politics, senior Republican Representative Paul Gosar has posted a violent video cartoon on the internet—which he edited—showing him cutting off the head of young, progressive Democratic Representative, Alexandria Ocasio-Cortez. When formally censured by a divided House, Gosar refused to apologize for his inappropriate sense of humor. The question raises itself: How much are we willing to accept?[93]

One Saturday afternoon—while I was working on this Father/Daughter project—I found myself observing a father and his two early-elementary-school-age children near me in the check-out line at the grocery store. The boy was standing on one side of his father, the girl on the other. Although it was a long wait, all three were calm and relaxed. Occasionally, the father would rub his son's shoulders or stroke his daughter's hair. She would turn around under his hand and lightly lean into him. It was affecting to see how connected and comfortable the three of them seemed to be, standing there together—the father giving equal loving attention to both children. The scene reminded me of a story told by a friend who grew up in a family that moved a lot during her childhood. Whenever they all came to a new place and met

---

[92] Joe Coscarelli & Liz Day, *The New York Times*, September 29 & October 2, 2021.
[93] Jonathan Weisman and Catie Edmonson, *The New York Times*, November 17, 2021.

new people, her father would introduce her and her sister and two brothers by name. Then, in a proud voice, he would add, "My daughters will be able to do anything my sons can do."

However slowly and gradually it happens, the key to change is to continue—with persistence and passion—to find ways to loosen the socially entrenched limited and limiting archetypal and historical reactions and attitudes that many fathers unconsciously hold towards their female off-spring— and toward the *feminine* in general. The task of a father is not to psychologically and emotionally devour his children or keep them from being born. A father's responsibility is to help his daughter develop her own spirit. Surely, the highest gift a father can give to his daughter is a solid sense of her worth, and of her unique individuality. When she has the knowledge that she is free to nurture her talents to do in the world what comes most naturally to her, a daughter has been given the essential tools to flourish, and to become the whole human being she has the potential to become.

References

Athanassakis, Apostolos N. trans. (1983) *Hesiod: Theogony, Works and Days, Shield*, Baltimore: John Hopkins University Press.

Ayers, Mary. (2003) *Mother-Infant Attachment and Psychoanalysis: The Eyes of Shame*, New York: Brunner-Routledge.

Demetrakopoulos, Stephanie A. (1979) "Hestia: Goddess of the Hearth: Notes on an Oppressed Archetype," *Spring*.

Goetz, Ruth and Augustus. (1975) *The Heiress*, New York: Dramatists Play Service.

Green, Liz. (1986) *The Astrology of Fate*, York Beach, Maine: Samuel Weiser, Inc.

Greenfield, Barbara. (1985) "The Archetypal Masculine: It's Manifestation in Myth, and Its Significance for Women," *The Father: Contemporary Jungian Perspectives*, ed. Andrew Samuels, London: Free Association Books.

James, Henry. (1962) *Washington Square*, New York: Dell Publishing Co., Inc.

Jung, C.G. (1953-1979) *The Collected Works* (Bollingen Series XX), 20 vols. Trans. R.F.C. Hull, Princeton, New Jersey: Princeton University Press.

Jung, C.G. (1940-1941) *Kindertraum Seminar: Winter,* (unpublished).

Jung, C.G. (1987) *Children's Dreams,* eds. Lorenz Jung and Maria Meyer-Grass, trans. Ernst Falzeder & Tony Woolfson, (Philomen Series), Olten: Walter-Verlag.

Kerenyi, Carl. (1958) *The Gods of the Greeks*, Middlesex: Penguin Books Ltd.

Kerenyi, Carl. (1980) "A Mythological Image of Girlhood," *Facing the Gods,* ed. James Hillman, Zurich: Spring Publications.

Kohut, Heinz. (1971) *The Analysis of the Self,* New York: International University Press.

McGuire, William and Hull, R.F.C. eds. (1980) *C.G. Jung Speaking: Interviews and Encounters*, London: Pan Books.

Nafisi, Azar. (2003) *Reading Lolita in Tehran: A Memoir in Books*, New York: Random House.

Nafisi, Azar. (2014) *The Republic of Imagination: America in Three Books*, New York: Viking.

Neumann, Erich. (1959) "Die Angst," *Studien aus dem C.G. Jung Institute*, Zurich: Rascher Verlag. Trans. Irene Gad in *Quadrant*, ed. Jeanne Walker, Vol.19, No.1, *Spring*, 1986.

Neumann, Erich. (1974) *The Great Mother: An Analysis of the Archetype*, (Bollingen Series XLVII), trans. Ralph Mannheim, Princeton, New Jersey: Princeton University Press.

Neumann, Erich. (1994) *The Fear of the Feminine: and Other Essays on Feminine Psychology*, (Bollingen Series LXI-4), trans: Boris Matthews, Esther Doughty, Eugene Rolf, and Michael Cullingworth, Princeton, New Jersey: Princeton University Press.

Stein, Murray. (1977) "The Devouring Father," *Fathers and Mothers: Five Papers on the Archetypal Background of Family Psychology*, ed. Patricia Berry, Zurich: Spring Publications.

Vitali, Augusto. (1977) "Saturn: The Transformation of the Father," *Fathers and Mothers: Five Papers on the Archetypal Background of Family Psychology*, ed. Patricia Berry, Zurich: Spring Publications.

Vries de, Ad. (1974) *Dictionary of Symbols and Imagery*, Amsterdam: North Holland Publishing Company.

Westover, Tara. (2018) *Educated: A Memoir*, New York: Random House.

Woolf, Virginia. (1938) *Three Guineas*, Orlando, Florida: Harcourt Brace Jovanovich, Inc.